zig-zagging
A MEMOIR

Loving Madly, Losing Badly—How Ziggy Saved My Life

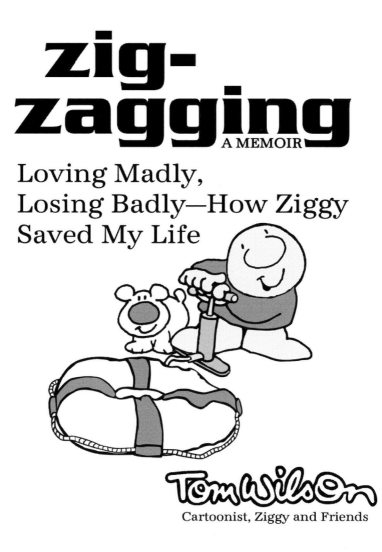

Tom Wilson

Cartoonist, Ziggy and Friends

Health Communications, Inc.
Deerfield Beach, Florida

www.hcibooks.com

**Library of Congress Cataloging-in-Publication Data
is available through the Library of Congress.**

© 2009 Tom Wilson and Olivia Rupprecht

ISBN-13: 978-0-7573-0793-5
ISBN-10: 0-7573-0793-0

Publisher: Health Communications, Inc.
        3201 S.W. 15th Street
        Deerfield Beach, FL 33442–8190

Cover design by Larissa Hise Henoch
Interior design and formatting by Lawna Patterson Oldfield

To Dad:

You will always be my greatest superhero

And to my beautiful and loving angel, Susan:

I will love you forever, Woozie

Contents

Acknowledgments

I have so many people to whom I owe my heartfelt appreciation for their expertise, help, and encouragement. And so, to Olivia Rupprecht, coauthor and dear friend; to Meredith Bernstein, dedicated agent and a true angel-unaware who believed; to Michele Matrisciani, my brilliant editor and muse; to Larissa Hise Henoch and Kim Weiss for going above and beyond; and to all of the truly talented and dedicated people at HCI who have made this such a wonderful publishing experience—I thank you all.

I would also like to offer a special acknowledgment, along with my sincere debt of gratitude, to Ms. Cindi Smith, a gentle woman who purchased that first and very special journal for me. Without her divinely inspired, unconditional act of kindness, this book would not exist.

Introduction

A WHILE BACK I was asked to write a business book that would "draw upon" my many years as a creative consultant and branding specialist. Well, true to form, that's not quite how things turned out. My initially simple and orderly plan for "Bringing life to the character of your business" ended up becoming a personally chaotic journey about "Bringing your character to the business of life."

As the cartoonist for Ziggy, I've spent a lot of one-on-one time with the little guy—since childhood to be exact. My dad, Tom Wilson, Sr., created him in the late 1960s. Ziggy has been my responsibility since the mid-1980s, and in the course of time I've come to realize that the character my father brought to life in his art has played a central role in my life and in the art of living it.

I believe that much of art and life are inextricably linked, that in art—as well as life—every masterpiece, like every great journey, must have a beginning and an end. What I failed to understand through so many chapters of my existence is that each end is also a beginning. *Everything*, in life and in art, exists in a constant state of becoming.

Our lives aren't composed like a headstone with a straight line that marks the date of the first breath we take to the last; the journey we're on is really a zigzagging series of unexpected detours. Every detour is a destination unto itself, and regardless of our plans, it's what we don't see coming that often affects us most.

One such detour I never saw coming brought me to where I am right now: Here. Alone, in what was once my father's house, attempting to return some order to the chaos that creation has left behind.

As a child, I called this place "home," but everything looked much different then. As an adult, several decades later, these walls define my artist's studio, a workshop where I create and bring new ideas to life. It's also headquarters for the two businesses I run in Cleveland: Ziggy and Friends, Inc., and Character Matters, Inc.

My home and family are in Cincinnati. On the map, the line separating and connecting the two cities of Cleveland and Cincinnati is a straight one. This line is about nine inches long and represents I-71. Size apparently *does* matter because those nine inches actually represent a mean distance of 250 miles, with a driving time of about four hours. It's basically a trip from the top of the state of Ohio to the bottom. I make this trip maybe twice a

. . . ON THE PATH OF LIFE THERE ARE A SERIES OF DETOURS . . . AND WE ALL GET REAL FRUSTRATED & IMPATIENT WHEN WE FEEL WE LEFT THE PATH . . .

. . . BUT WHAT IF THE **REAL** PATH OF LIFE IS ALL OF THOSE DETOURS PUT TOGETHER!

. . . AND INSTEAD OF LEARNING THE **REAL** LESSONS, . . . WE MISSED THEM BECAUSE WE WERE TOO BUSY BEING FRUSTRATED & IMPATIENT!

~ZIGGY

month, packing in as much as possible in a couple of days. So as you might guess, I've lost count of how many times I've gone back and forth, up and down, this straight line over the years.

Taking one final pass through every room of the old house, I switch off the lights and lock the front door behind me as I leave.

In the daylight hours, when I usually arrive, creators and muses are hard at work foreshadowing bright futures through the bright ideas they create—only for memories of heroes and angels to flash back from an ever-dimming past when I take my leave at night, as I often do. Balanced within this space between night and day, where the darkness meets the light, is that engaging place called shadow. I walk through it now.

As I head for my car, I'm still surprised at how suddenly dusk can come, especially at this time of the year. I load my suitcase and laptop computer into the back and hop into the driver's seat of my minivan—not exactly the Batmobile I dreamed of driving as a boy, but even big boys can still dream their little dreams, and tonight is a night made for dreaming.

Starting the engine, I'm joined by my thoughts and my trusted copilot Ziggy to help guide me down the road ahead. And then I notice a forgotten light reaching out through the shadows from a basement window to meet the blazing headlights of my Batmobile.

I'm in a hurry to get home so I just keep driving.

Winding down the long, wooded driveway, I glance in the rearview mirror, and as that light recedes from view, a dim memory grows brighter; I remember waiting for another light, from a different car, to shine through that same window, so very long ago . . .

BACKWARD . . .

IT'S A FRIDAY NIGHT, more than thirty-five years ago, and I'm sitting on the green cracked vinyl sofa in our basement, anxiously waiting for a beam of light to shine through the windows and onto the wall above our old TV. My twelve-year-old body is exhausted from five straight days of learning, chasing young love, and hours upon hours of swim team practice, but I don't dare fall asleep. Tonight is the night I've waited for all week.

It seems like forever, then at last! The headlights of Dad's car herald his arrival home.

My mom and sister have gone to bed, and finally I hear my father's heavy footsteps coming down the basement stairs. We share our tired smiles as he takes up his position on the maroon shag carpeting and our midnight "Creature Feature" begins. It's here in this room, with *Godzilla* on the tube, that the two most influential characters in my life lie spread out before me. The first is my superhero as well as the most brilliant man I will ever know. He's gotten comfortable after a long day, whittled down to his boxer shorts, a rumpled dress shirt, and loosened tie. With a cigarette in one hand, a pen in the other, he's drawing the second character: a short, little bald guy with a big nose—Ziggy.

It doesn't matter that the movie completely sucks or that my dad and I are so physically beat we'll never see the end of the show. No, those things don't matter. What does is that this is *our* time, and we both know how much it means to each other without ever having to say so.

I fight the urge to sleep while the great man in his underwear works long into the night, drawing beneath the television's projection of one classic character as he continues to create another. Ultimately, as Godzilla wreaks chaos on Tokyo, my tired eyes fix upon the steady stream of smoke from Dad's burning Kool menthol gracefully meandering up, up, and away, taking my consciousness along with it.

As I fall asleep, I don't think about the funny little character he draws by night. I haven't yet experienced the pressures of syndication deadlines, and I don't know that *Ziggy* has only recently entered the world in eighteen newspapers and is struggling to survive. All I know is that these brief, special times Dad and I spend together make everything else that's taking place in our respective worlds stop, so that he might share this part of his life with me.

We often shared another ritual, one memory that I treasure to this day. Many weekends, Dad and I would go to breakfast at our local Big Boy restaurant. It was here, again, that Ziggy always joined us. We both knew the routine. As soon as the server brought Dad his first cup of coffee and he lit his first cigarette, we turned over our placemats to play our SAVE ZIGGY! game.

At the time I never imagined it would ultimately become an example of art imitating life.

This game of ours always began the same. Dad would draw a picture of Ziggy happily strolling along, unaware of some horrible misfortune about to befall him. Ziggy might be zooming off a cliff, walking unknowingly into an open manhole, or oblivious to a meteor plummeting head-on his way. After Ziggy had been drawn into one of these dire circumstances, Dad would flip the placemat around, hand me his pen, and say, "Tommy, it's time for you to SAVE ZIGGY!"

The game had only two rules: I could not use my first idea, and I could not use any obvious solution. Consequently, I would always come to Ziggy's rescue by drawing upon some of the most elaborately creative strategies a twelve-year-old boy could imagine. I had no idea that what seemed like just a game to me was actually my father's contrived training exercise in creative problem solving.

I recall one specific occasion when Dad and I were at our favorite Big Boy restaurant, playing our game of SAVE ZIGGY! On this particular morning, instead of coming up with some creative solution to rescue Ziggy, I attempted to draw a *perfect* Ziggy to impress my dad. When I proudly turned the placemat around to show him, he blew out the smoke of his cigarette between him and the drawing, shook his head, and said, "You're pootzelling too much, Tom!"

"Huh?"

At first I feared this might become some segue into a good old father-son talk referring to all the time I'd been spending lately in the shower, but much to my relief, he instead told me a story about his days in art school as a student.

Dad had an old Russian art teacher he really admired. One time in drawing class his instructor walked around behind the students, looking over their shoulders, watching them work. When he came to Dad, he walked right past him with hardly a glance. Although Dad was never arrogant about his abilities, he did believe himself to be a much better artist than the person next to him, who was getting all of the teacher's attention. Now this amply bothered Dad so that he worked and reworked his own drawing, trying to emulate the style of his teacher, hoping to gain his attention and approval.

The teacher finally came to Dad's easel. As my father looked up expectantly, the teacher ripped Dad's drawing from his pad, threw it to the floor, and yelled, "Stop pootzelling, Vilson!"

To which Dad replied, "Huh?"

In his thick Russian accent, the teacher told him, "Is not vat you draw, Vilson. Is not *how vell* you draw. Is *vhere* you draw from that makes *difference*."

Dad went on to tell me that the teacher defined "pootzelling" as trying too hard to create something into what it really is not, and in so doing, sacrificing that something's originality, its true character. Dad said that people can "pootzel" in life as well as in art.

I might've only been a kid, but I got the point.

When the server finally arrived with my usual plate of chocolate chip pancakes, instead of picking up the placemat as I always did to preserve our sketches, I left it on the table so that the plate would cover what no longer held any pride for me but something I was instead ashamed to have drawn.

The lesson that my father served up, and that Ziggy has always personified, has been an important guidepost for me over the years: it's okay to be imperfect as long as we honor our true character instead of trying to live up to some preconceived image or perceived expectation of being someone other than who we really are. That's far easier said than done, yet my father lived it by example, personally and professionally, and Ziggy has reinforced this truth since he was brought to life many decades ago.

Dad believed that anything we can imagine creating, we are capable of achieving, as long as it's conceived in an inspired moment and carried by our passion within. In addition to creating one of the world's most successful and beloved cartoon characters, Dad was one of the earliest and most innovative pioneers in the industry of modern character licensing. Through his association with American Greetings Corporation, he founded Those Characters From Cleveland, the character licensing company responsible for creating, developing, and licensing such well-known properties as Strawberry Shortcake, Care Bears, and many others.

Even so, the greatness of the man in my mind comes not only from his spectacular accomplishments, but also because he embraced life with a rare zest for living and gave the best of himself to the world—and his family.

Born to a coal miner and his schoolteacher wife, Dad was a tall, lean, engaging young man who grew up in Panther Lick Run, Pennsylvania. When I look at his old photos, I see a sparkling wisdom in his eyes and an infectious, dimpled smile. Dad's character was defined in the contrast between his older brother, Charlie, a boy genius and war hero who died far too young, and his younger brother, Ralph, the darling of their parents and very talented in his own right. Dad believed that as a middle child, he had to work twice as hard as his siblings and excel in his own areas to gain his share of familial attention.

As a kid he loved to draw and discovered early on that he had a natural skill for cartooning. He worked at the local newspaper setting type for the printers and designing advertisements for local businesses. In the army, he drew caricatures of his military buddies, and even in art school his paintings and drawings were a unique amalgam of both fine art and cartooning.

After leaving the army in the early 1950s, Dad attended the Pittsburgh Institute of Art on the GI Bill. It was here that he met his very talented wife, Carol, and upon graduation, they moved to Cleveland to look for work as artists.

It was in Cleveland in the mid-1950s that Dad went to work at American Greetings as a greeting card artist. Assigned to a new department in charge of creating a line of humorous studio cards,

AG Highbrows, Dad literally began the line by designing their logo and drawing the very first card in 1956. Up until then, greeting cards had always been the "Roses are red, violets are blue" variety. They basically consisted of scenic landscapes and bouquets of flowers partnered with saccharine sweet prose—a social expression including a beautiful painting senders could never paint and flowery lines of poetry senders would never be able to compose themselves.

It wasn't long before Dad was promoted to art director of Highbrow. These Highbrow cards were something new, clever, distinctive. Instead of simply offering some pretty words and a pretty picture to go with them, Highbrow cards were designed for maximum communication from sender to receiver and were meant to appeal to the largest audience possible. Humor was an important trademark of these cards, but behind the humor was some very serious thinking.

One of the primary devices used was the development of a character, or characters, that both sender and receiver could readily identify with. These were neuter characters, for lack of a better term, and were intentionally ambiguous and nondescript so that the card's message would seem to be directly from the sender. The idea was to design characters that were generic enough to appeal to the largest segment of the card-sending public.

Another important strategy was to have these characters speak their humorous lines directly to the card's recipient. This assured not only a direct communication, but also allowed the character to be more closely associated with the card's sender. Generally, these were called "Me to You" cards. These devices are still widely used today; it's a time-tested method, backed by billions of dollars in sales over the years.

Since Dad was intimately involved in the evolution of these cards, it's no coincidence that when he finally developed Ziggy in the mid- to late-1960s, he incorporated many of these successful communication devices into the character. Ziggy is simple; nothing gets in the way of the message. He's friendly and lovable. If this guy shows up at your door, you're not going to get out the shotgun. You're going to welcome him in because he's looking right at you with complete sincerity and all the goodness in his heart.

If you read a lot of comic strips, and I certainly don't mean this critically, it's almost as if you're looking into another world or at a TV screen. Reading the paper and seeing these little frames is like peeking through a window of the character's house, watching them do their thing. Ziggy, however, is conscious of the reader. He always has been. Whether in a greeting card or a comic strip, he's looking back at you, and you can't help but think, "Hey, he's aware of me, too." You're not just voyeuristically looking in on him; he knows you're there and he appreciates your presence. He wants you to be comfortable and happy while he delivers what he's supposed to give.

A while back I asked Dad where this idea came from, and he said, "I used to watch those Laurel and Hardy movies, and every time Stanley would do something stupid, you'd see Ollie look out at you from the screen, and roll his eyes as if to say, "I know you're there; isn't this guy a dope?""

Originally, Dad created a comical character that looked very much like Ziggy but was an elevator operator who commented on current events in much the same way an editorial cartoon would. Dad shopped it around the syndicates, trying to sell it, but received little interest from them. One editor at King Features Syndicate, whom Dad remembered as a very heavy, short woman, didn't like that Ziggy was short and fat, and reprimanded him with the admonishment: "It's not funny to make fun of people who are short and fat!"

Ironically, this editor, whose job it was to recognize the strength in characters, unknowingly fell victim to Ziggy's superior ability to invoke identification with his reader.

Dad put Ziggy on the back burner for several years, which was just as well because he'd agreed to more responsibility and was busy initiating and developing many other innovative and creative concepts through his role at American Greetings. One of these concepts was a series of small, humorous, cardlike books, that were published under the name Sunbeam Library. Apparently, his staff was extremely overworked while trying to meet the deadline for completion of this project, so Dad pitched in and illustrated one of these small books himself, and brought out Ziggy as its character.

The book was titled *When You're Not Around*, and it sold an amazing half a million copies. By an equally amazing coincidence, a wonderful woman named Kathy Andrews purchased a copy. She bought it for her husband, Jim, who was busy traveling with his partner, John McMeel. They had a fledgling comic syndicate by the name of Universal Press Syndicate.

Jim Andrews loved the little book and Ziggy so much he immediately contacted Dad at American Greetings and asked if they could carry Ziggy. At that time, they had acquired only one feature, a little-known comic strip done by some college kid named Garry Trudeau. So *Doonesbury* and *Ziggy* launched Universal Press Syndicate and helped make it the largest comic strip syndicate in the world today.

Once *Ziggy* became syndicated with Universal Press Syndicate, American Greetings president, Irving Stone, offered to buy Ziggy from Dad. Dad refused. After *Ziggy* had been in the papers for about a year, American Greetings licensed him for use in greeting cards, and *Ziggy* became one of their greatest licensed card lines ever, selling more than 50 million cards per year.

Not bad for a guy of modest beginnings and a GI Bill education. Of course, I was just a toddler when his career at American Greetings was in its early stages, and I have no personal recollections of it. Still, I *do* remember other things about growing up surrounded by my parents' art because Mom and Dad were both gifted painters.

I also distinctly remember that in their first house they shared an art studio in the basement, which seemed to me like a secret place of creation, where the alchemic brew of tobacco smoke and turpentine mingled with shadow and mystery.

One of my earliest and most vivid memories is sitting at the breakfast table on a weekend morning, reading the back of a cereal box, and hearing heavy footsteps clomp up the basement stairs behind the old blue door that led to the kitchen. Peeking over the top of Tony the Tiger, I'd watch the door creak open as my weary father emerged, still wearing the same clothes he'd had on the night before. It was always the same: My father would kiss my mother at the kitchen counter as she handed him his coffee. He'd light a cigarette, walk over to the table, and give me a smoky smile along with an affectionate tussle to my white-blond hair.

The smell of cigarette smoke was familiar, but each time my father came up from those stairs, he brought with him an odd mixture of strange and intriguing odors.

One night, just before my parents took me upstairs and put me to bed, I noticed the door leading to the basement had been left ajar. I waited until the old house became quiet, then sneaked downstairs. My parents knew they had an unusually curious boy, so they'd warned me: *Dangerous things are down there, bad things that can hurt a little boy.* They told me never to go down those stairs, and I never did . . . until that night.

I stood before the old blue door, slowly pulled it open, and took my first step into the blackness. I didn't dare switch on the light, and my fear grew in proportion to the thickening darkness and mysterious fumes that enveloped me with every hesitant step deeper into the abyss. Unknown dangers lurked below, but they couldn't really hurt a little boy, right? After all, he was going to be Batman!

I remember touching the cracked, peeling, yet reassuring image of my favorite superhero printed on the front of my Dr. Denton pajamas, and quietly summoning the forces of good against the forces of darkness, I whispered, "To the Batcave!"

On the final step, creaky wood gave way to cold concrete. I can still feel the musty dampness in the stone shooting through the

peeling plastic pads on the bottom of my flannel-covered feet. Each step was an unforgiving, loud, scraping noise as my thin little legs shuffled farther into the cavelike darkness.

Suddenly, I heard a *click* from the switch at the top of the stairs. Just enough light streamed down to illuminate a triangular door directly under the staircase. I rushed into that little room, a storage area, and sat quiet as a mouse. Boxes of familiar Christmas decorations surrounded me, which I found strangely comforting while I listened to my father's descending footsteps on the creaking wood above me.

From my little hiding place, I peeked through a crack in the door, and with the second *click* of a switch, my father unveiled his mysterious world of creation.

I watched, transfixed, as this man I so deeply loved stood before a huge blank canvas, mixing odd-smelling liquids with the colors he squeezed from the many silver metal tubes scattered around him.

Then there was a third and final *click*: the familiar, thin metallic sound of a lighter. My father lit a cigarette. He selected a brush from the many sticking out of a blue Maxwell House coffee can on the paint-covered table beside him.

And in that moment I witnessed the process of creation. His broad slashing strokes splashed color and spirit onto the canvas, like the sorcerer's apprentice magically conducting the elements of nature, until, eventually, the steady stream of smoke from his cigarette carried me away to sleep.

The next morning I woke up in my own bed, confused. Had it all been a dream? Reluctantly, I went downstairs to breakfast, not sure if I was in trouble, or even if I actually *had* disobeyed my parents the night before and should be feeling guilty.

My mother was unusually quiet as I softly padded into the kitchen, so I sat down at the table, poured milk and cereal into the bowl, and hid behind Tony the Tiger's box.

As usual I heard my father's heavy footsteps ascending the basement stairs. As usual the old blue door creaked opened and my father kissed my mother as she handed him his coffee. As usual he lit a cigarette, walked over to the table, and looked down at his little boy.

I sheepishly peered up from behind the box, offering my most practiced innocent smile, and waited for my father's smoky smile and a tussle to my hair in return.

After what seemed like an eternity, I received them both—only my father unexpectedly paused in midtussle and pulled a tangled piece of gold tinsel from my hair. I remember that damning evidence dangling between my guilty expression and the robust image of Tony the Tiger confirming my crime with a wink, a hearty thumbs-up, and a resounding *GRRRRRRREAT!!*

Then my father smiled, and he led me to the old blue door, which he'd left wide-open. As we walked down the stairs together, Dad held my hand. Who needed Batman now? My favorite super-hero was right there, taking me down to his studio, and explain-ing everything about this magical place in painstaking detail.

Eventually we ended up in front of the triangular door under the stairs. My father told me to open it and I did. He pulled the cord to the bare lightbulb hanging inside. The Christmas decora-tions were gone. The little storage room had been thoroughly cleaned, furnished with a small chair and table.

On top of the table was a fresh box of 64 Crayola crayons and several new drawing pads. On the wall at the back of my new room was a freshly painted, hand-lettered sign that read: BATCAVE.

From that day, what began as a zigzagging trek into the dark unknown became a place of transformation and light. For years to come, my father and I would descend together into the shadowy, creative space of that wonderful basement art studio. Admittedly, my own drawing back then was pretty much relegated to the refrigerator door, especially since wall space was at a premium in our cramped little first house in Cleveland.

While Mom painted vibrant abstracts and was an equally tal-ented portrait painter, Dad preferred doing portraits that were, in reality, more like character studies. Those had the greatest impact on me. I couldn't even go to the bathroom without looking up from my Batman comic book into the eyes of weary, toil-blackened coal miners, long-forgotten jazz musicians, corrupt politicians, and salvation-slinging preachers.

Perspective can cross time and space, granting depth and dimension to everything we see and do. What I observed as a kid were really cool pictures of coal miners, musicians, and funny-looking preachers and politicians. Stepping back now, as an adult and professional artist myself, I can't help but notice the dark-sided nature of the compelling characters he illustrated. They were like two strikingly different sides to the same coin.

The father I knew, and the man practically everyone else knew, had all of the admirable qualities represented by the characters in his work—strength, genius, and purpose—yet in his art he chose to reveal the negative counterparts of those fine traits:

Strength in the vacant faces of his downtrodden coal miners, but strength relegated to a short and miserable lifetime of health-wasting labor.

Genius in his old jazz musicians, but genius neglected, long forgotten, and unappreciated.

Lost purpose in his podium-gripping preachers and corrupt, alcoholic politicians, condemning souls with hellfire and damnation and saving them with phony Square Deals and rubber chickens in every pot.

This brings to mind something that the writer Herman Hesse once said: "If you hate a person, you hate something in him that is part of yourself. What isn't part of ourselves doesn't disturb us."

I think a lot of truth is in that observation. It's like a knee-jerk reaction to push the Creature from the Black Lagoon back into the stagnant swamp we've just managed to escape, or inappropriate laughter slipping free like a nervous tic from our own internal discomfort. This isn't really so different from what Dad did with these caricatures, inviting us to laugh uneasily with him as he mocked the twin monsters of good character gone bad, and great potential made waste.

As a kid in the '60s and '70s, I used characters portrayed in television shows to draw comparisons. I always felt like Opie to my dad's Andy. Dad seemed to have that same countrified wisdom, which he'd dispense to me in a casual voice, accompanied by the tussle of my hair (of course that damn cigarette he was holding was still a problem). To me, my father was a hero who truly embodied everything good about being a man.

Today, Mom and Dad's paintings no longer hang side by side on the same wall or even in the same house, but I'm still struck by the dissimilarity of their artwork that surrounded me while growing up. I remember Mom's beautiful portraits of her young family juxtaposed against Dad's dark portraits of characters we'd never met, and hopefully never would. Mom still paints, and while her skill is greater than ever, her subject matter has changed dramatically over time. In years past, she often painted turbulent abstractions in blues. Now she paints peaceful and elegant still lifes.

It's been a long time since Dad held a paintbrush in his hand. Yet his images still reach from the past like a gnarled finger tapping my shoulder, pointing to where I presently stand on matters of character in every aspect of my life.

Tomorrow's dreams are dependent upon our ability to survive Today's realities, and todays realities can only be survived if we keep alive tomorrows dreams.

— Wilson

DON'T WORRY ABOUT TOMORROW
UNTIL YOU MAKE IT THROUGH TODAY!!

—Ziggy

Thinking back, I can't help but wonder how the rest of the father-son Big Boy weekend crowd perceived my dad and me. I can still see the other boys in their Little League uniforms postgame, talking sports with their own dads. This was quite a contrast to the skinny blond-haired boy at the other table, nodding in adoring silence, bobbing to dodge the burning end of that eternal cigarette in Dad's gesturing hand, while both of us scribbled away on our coffee-stained paper placemats.

I loved those moments when it was just Dad, Zig, and me. In hindsight, I realize those were times of true growth for all three of us, when Dad and I would draw upon our thoughts and feelings about Ziggy and life, and in the process draw out our thoughts and feelings about each other.

Over time, I began to view Ziggy not only as my father's successful brainchild, but also as a very real sibling I could relate to. He was like the little brother who "made good." Growing up together, Zig and I shared many of the same experiences that helped shape our characters. Within both of us resided a lot of our father—Ziggy as art in a two-dimensional way, and me as his offspring in three-dimensional life.

Ziggy enjoyed phenomenal success that continued to grow with each passing year—mass syndication, greeting cards, countless licensing deals for his image, even an Emmy for his *Ziggy's Gift*

Christmas animation special (first released in 1982, now on DVD)—and, of course, I continued to grow up, although without such spectacular achievements.

Unfortunately, however, the time eventually came when SAVE ZIGGY! was no longer a game but a grim reality. Dad was only in his fifties when he began to suffer from serious health issues. By then *Ziggy* had a healthy audience and had become very serious business. Ziggy needed to continue. So as Dad became increasingly less able to do the work, the more I stepped in to write, to draw, and ultimately to take complete responsibility for *Ziggy*. Since my initial involvement, which began in the mid-1980s, I have been drawing and writing the lines for Ziggy.

Today the two most influential characters of my childhood are still in my life, and both are integral parts of the person I continue to become. However, while one character has been "saved," is alive, well, and visited each day in the comic pages by 75 million people, the other, despite the best efforts of many over the years, currently resides in a care facility, and I visit him whenever I can. I love my dad, and in my heart I know he will always love me.

Years of struggle with health issues and a hard-won battle with the not-so-Kool consequences of too many Joe Camels (lung cancer) have taken their toll on the man Dad once was.

However, Tom Wilson, The Man, will always be with us through the life he brought to his art. To me, in art and in life, my dad will always be one of the world's most gifted creators and the greatest superhero I have ever known.

As for Ziggy, he's still the quintessential little guy in the big world—clumsy and so insecure that the only thing he's sure of is that he's unsure of himself. Yet throughout it all he retains the wide-eyed wonder of a child, or a deer caught in life's headlights. We see Ziggy dealing with life's problems day after day, but he still manages to get out of bed to be with us each morning in our newspapers.

In the many years I've been drawing Ziggy, he's pretty much grown beyond his loser status and achieved inspirational-character standing. People often tell me how Ziggy has been with them through their good times and their bad times. They say that Ziggy always deals with the problems life keeps throwing his way, making them feel not so bad or alone while dealing with problems of their own.

Ziggy is a humble, everyday hero whose own journey began decades ago. Launched in just a handful of newspapers scattered across the country, today he appears in syndication around the world.

It's been said that a little character can go a long way, and Ziggy has definitely gone the distance since I sat on that old green vinyl couch, watching Dad draw him to life as he sat on the maroon shag carpeting in our basement—where a distant light continues to reach out from the shadows.

UPWARD...

T HE DRIVEWAY IS now behind me, and I'm making my way onto I-71, a not-so-super highway that's become so familiar to me over the years it seems to have a character of its own. Once again, it's leading me from Cleveland, the birthplace of Superman and other boyhood heroes, to Cincinnati, my current hood and birthplace of my own two super boys.

On the trip north to Cleveland, I'm usually in a rush and thinking of making meetings, beginning new projects, or meeting my deadlines. My mind is continually at work the entire way: planning, preparing, and contemplating the future. For me, this has been the road most traveled by and, in many ways, it *has* made all the difference. Lost in my thoughts, I ultimately find that I reach the end of my journey before I know it, and am always amazed at how quickly the time has passed.

However, on the return journey home, such as now, time takes on an entirely different character as I leave my mind behind, and a different spirit joins me in the driver's seat. Sensing something precious missing in my life, the draw of my family makes every mile seem endless and each minute feel like forever.

I'm smiling now as I recall the family vacations my wife and I took with our kids when they were small. I remember Susan calmly sitting beside me as I drove, leaning over to kiss me on the cheek, telling me to relax as Miles and Sam fought in the backseat like archenemies the whole way there.

Then, all I could think about was getting us to our destination as quickly as possible.

Now, I wish that journey had never ended.

In looking back to what seems a lifetime ago, what emerges from the shadows most clearly is that what I really missed was the most important point of all: The journey we travel together is never really about *getting to* our destination point. It is about the process of *getting to the point* of the journey itself.

Confucius once said, "A journey of a thousand miles begins with a single step." But when you stop to think about just how many steps we actually take on our journeys—all you may have to go through to get where you're going, not to mention what you might step *in* along the way—well, that oft-coined phrase of "going nowhere fast" doesn't seem so out of line.

I'm merging with I-71 South from the on-ramp. Dead-straight and steely-gray, like the shaft of a sculptor's chisel, this seemingly endless highway cuts through the flat, Ohio vista toward some elusive vanishing point along the illuminated horizon.

It feels as if I'm in a race with the setting sun to the horizon, driving this chisel home, where another light in another window will still be shining, and my own hero's welcome awaits. I can live with that. It's kind of nice to be on the flip side of the generational coin, to reach that place where we can observe childhood from the perspective of adulthood and realize that life is a great, eternal circle that repeats itself in different, yet not always so different, ways . . .

* * *

Our "wonder years" aren't always exactly wonderful, and sometimes it can seem like a wonder that we manage to survive them. After all, this is a time when "finding yourself" can be pretty difficult because you don't know where to look, when "getting in touch with yourself" means something entirely different, and "taking a closer look at yourself" usually has something to do with checking in the bathroom mirror for zits.

Like many teenagers, I first began to explore the undiscovered country of my own character, and what I perceived the adult world to be, about the time I was preparing to graduate from high school and enter college. I remember feeling an incredible urgency

to find out just who I was and to find it out fast. I'd hurriedly try on this or that characteristic, which seemed popular and valuable at the time, only to quickly discard it because the trait seemed completely uninteresting and it didn't fit. I was like a kid at Christmas whose mom ordered him to try on the hand-knitted sweater Aunt Mildred lovingly spent three months making, before he can open the really cool packages under the tree that may contain something "As Seen On TV!"

Fortunately, time is a great teacher, and in 1975 I managed to graduate from high school. From there I went to college at Miami University in southern Ohio. Here, fate kindly introduced me to yet another remarkable hero: the woman who would one day become my wife.

I met Susan Shephard in Life Drawing my sophomore year, and she became my main incentive to be in class. I belonged to a fraternity and 8:30 in the morning seemed awfully early to wake up, sit in front of some naked old man, and get motivated to draw. Although the class was called Life Drawing, I think the onus was definitely on the students to put a little life into the drawing because it certainly didn't seem to be coming from the models.

Nevertheless, I knew right then and there, that *this* was the woman I was going to marry. Besides having fallen madly in love with her, Susan came from a very different family background than my own, and one I found enormously appealing. I was raised in a creatively rich environment, which didn't always lend itself to traditional family values. Susan, by contrast, was born into a family that prized stability and the deeply rooted ideals of hearth and home. I couldn't help but desire to know, to hold for myself, some of what she had, which her family so generously shared with me.

Susan brought some much-needed order and focus to a life that had previously known its share of chaos and perhaps more free-dom than was entirely healthy. I'm sure this impacted my decision then, and the choices and decisions I would eventually come to make, as we traveled along together through the life and love we were about to create.

So being mad and impetuous at age twenty, I asked this beau-tiful woman to marry me. For being a naive kid, asking Susan "The Question" was one of the smartest things I'd ever done—or would ever do. Believe me, at that age I couldn't really be credited with too many smart things—although I did win the all-campus beer-chugging championship for my fraternity, complete with a trophy proudly exhibited in the lobby of the frat house. Well, until the house burned down years later. (For the record, I was away at the time of the rather large fire that did the place in, along with my prized trophy.)

While I chugged my way through college, Susan finished her degree a year ahead of me. As a graduation gift, I gave her the only present I could afford at the time: *me* (fortunately, she didn't try to exchange it). I proposed to her that same summer and we were married immediately. As luck would have it, her father just happened to be a minister, and he married us in their living room (*also* for the record, no shotgun was involved). I think our entire wedding came in well under $200, the most expensive part being the shrimp tray from Kroger's grocery store,

which *also,* as luck would have it, had the same expiration date as our wedding day.

At this point, I decided that rather than pursue graphic design, I would study fine art and illustration, thanks to my exposure to so many art history classes I loved. Since childhood, I'd known I was an artist and loved to paint, but increasingly, the completion of any painting became ancillary to the idea behind it and the process of its creation. *The idea,* that's where the excitement and the fun have always been for me, and I have a basement of unfinished paintings to prove it (procrastination means never getting around to saying you're sorry). I actually became an okay painter, but my love, *my passion,* centered on the art of the idea and not the art per se.

In Art History I discovered that pretty pictures are not just pretty pictures at all, no matter how well they're painted, and depending on your perspective, even those we see as "not so pretty" can have a unique beauty behind them. I grew to appreciate the ideas behind the art, as well as the inspiration behind the ideas, and in my senior year I transferred to Boston University, where I changed my major from Graphic Design to Fine Art and Illustration.

So Susan and I went to Boston, had our honeymoon at the Hyatt, looked for a suitably bohemian apartment—read: cheap—

found one in a particularly "cultural" section of town—read: *very* cheap—and I went about the process of becoming a starving artist while finishing my degree. Susan, who had quite a talent for graphics and design, was able to land a job in her chosen profession and support us through the duration.

Susan brought so many positive things into my life, and after she saw me through graduation from Boston University, I found a great job in Gotham City itself—read: New York. One particularly memorable event involved the day we moved there and met an old homeless man.

There we were, moving to our first apartment in midtown Manhattan, and I was attempting to maneuver a U-Haul truck full of furniture through those crazy, narrow, one-way streets. Susan sat beside me in the front seat, and we had our dog, Angus, with us. Finally we arrived in front of our building. Believe me, after fighting rush-hour traffic through the city, sitting on the edge of my seat the whole time, then trying to negotiate a Godzilla-sized truck down this very narrow street while frantically searching for a nonexistent parking place, my nerves were *shot*. We were both hot, frustrated, exhausted, and the last thing we needed was to try to figure out how to park a gigantic U-Haul on East Twenty-fifth Street between Second and Third Avenues.

The curses spouting from my mouth were in sharp contrast

to Susan's silent prayers, and I was about ready to "lose it" when I heard a tap and a gravelly voice outside my window. I warily rolled it down a few inches. A weathered, bearded face of a homeless man greeted me. He was shabby, old, had the stereotypical bottle in a paper bag sticking out of his pocket. He smiled a big toothless grin, nodded at us, and started pointing, enthusiastically waving me backward.

Now, bear in mind this was our first real experience with the city, and New York was the last place in the world I would have expected help from a stranger. But very calmly the old guy stood

aside and guided us into a spot I hadn't seen; one that I swear hadn't been there a few seconds earlier.

Even as I got out of the truck I could smell him. He looked at me with such a gentle expression, and I expressed how genuinely grateful we were for his help. I offered him money, but he wouldn't take it. He offered me his bottle—

And damned if I didn't take a drink.

He smiled at us and then walked away.

When I got back into the U-Haul Susan patted my hand and said, "He was an angel unaware." At that point I had to agree with her: angels unaware really do exist. Like detours, by simple and unconditional acts of kindness, they can change any journey, even if we don't realize it at the time.

Anyway, Susan and I moved to Manhattan, basically exchanging one cockroach-infested apartment for another. Susan got a job at the Stewart, Tabori & Chang publishing firm, working under one of the greatest book designers of our day, Nai Chang. Sadly, soon after Susan began working, Nai's wife became seriously ill from cancer, and Susan found herself running the department in his absence while he stayed home to care for his wife.

One nice perk Susan enjoyed was attending promotional launch parties for select books, and she was able to bring me along. We were still basically broke, and not only was the food free, but it was catered by company president Andy Stewart's wife, Martha, an enterprising businesswoman who would later go on to craft a pretty famous name of her own. When I met her, she seemed nice to me, but then *"It's a good thing"* she didn't know the pockets of my army jacket were stuffed with her canapés.

Meanwhile, I'd bought a tie, got a haircut, and began my dream job at a New York City toy company where I got to play in a new creative sandbox by designing and creating new toy ideas and characters. The company was small, so I pretty much had free rein to let my ideas come to life as often as possible or as far as the budget would allow. I had a wonderful art department and worked with a terrific boss, Stephanie Janis, who's still a good friend and currently one of the country's top doll designers.

Originally I'd planned to use toy development as a springboard to join an ad agency, where I would claw my way to the top, again to create ideas. I foresaw myself as the Darrin Stephens of the 1980s in a world of Madison Avenue Larry Tates, with my beautiful, bewitching wife beside me, making everything seem magically easier than it is. But life took another turn and, about a year or so into my Amtoy job, I started playing on the side with ideas for a cartoon character of my own. Honestly, I still can't figure out what compelled me to do this. It's possible that the idea to create my own cartoon might have come from my adulation of Dad, but strange as it sounds, my character really just seemed to make his presence known to me, and I *had* to draw him to life.

He was a caveman-type character named UG. He just sort of appeared one day, and I decided to let him stick around for a while. It's funny, I remember Dad saying the same thing about Ziggy. That's the thing about inspired characters, it's almost as if they have a consciousness or mind of their own but need a little help from some dumb guy who can draw.

I went about developing UG more and more, to the point where I felt he had evolved enough to go public. Since I had some understanding of newspaper comic syndication, I pitched *UG* as a children's strip to the syndicate that carried *Ziggy*. I recall at the time an actual debate was going on about whether or not newspaper comics were for children or for adults. My experience with *UG* eventually taught me that, for the most part, they're for adults—or more specifically, perhaps, the child in every adult as opposed to the adult in every child.

"UG" had a good run of about three years. I think he was in seventy to eighty papers. Not enormous papers, but essentially I was officially a syndicated cartoonist. This was a terrific point in my life.

People magazine did an article on Dad and me, which was a real thrill. A father and son having separate syndicated cartoons was something of a novelty, and I remember that magazine shoot as being one of the proudest days of my life.

So, there I was, a Boy Wonder at twenty-seven on the road to making my first million by thirty, exactly as planned. And there Dad and I were in *People* magazine—a two-page spread, Dad and I sitting side by side with a big picture of Ziggy behind him and a picture of UG behind me. While I was the Boy Wonder, I never doubted that Dad still was, and always would be, Batman. Together we were cartooning crusaders, minus the capes.

I swear, as I think back, when he and I were painting side by side, drawing our characters for this shoot in *People* magazine, I thought all my dreams had come true and I had finally "arrived."

People — Heirs

DRAWING ON HIS INHERITANCE, TOM WILSON JR. UNVEILS A ZIGGYFIED, HARD-LUCK HERO NAMED UG

If you are a comic-strip devotee and live in the right place, you have noticed a new character ambling across your funny papers lately. A big, bumbling bundle of fur, he's a lovable hunk called UG. What you probably don't know is that the newcomer is closely related to an older and beloved denizen of the strips, a small, oafish blob named Ziggy. The connection lies in the signatures on their panels. Ziggy owes his existence to Tom Wilson Sr., 53, and UG is the creation of Wilson's 27-year-old son, Tom Jr.

As far as authorities in the cartoon business can tell, the Wilsons are the

CONTINUED

HULLO ...i'M ZIGGY

... AND I'M TOM

...ARE WE PEOPLE YET ?

NO ! I'M TOM

Tom Sr. (left) and Tom Jr. call Ziggy and UG "neutral characters" who, while male, have no age or ethnic affiliation.

Viewing that photograph through the lens of hindsight, I now see two men with their alter egos drawn behind them—and yet, don't we all have a hidden place within our characters where our secret identities patiently lie in wait until there's a need for them to emerge? UG, I've come to realize, was in many ways that to me, especially how he always timidly tiptoed from the shadow of his cave, flinching because of the bright light, and then withdrew back into the safe anonymity of darkness.

UG was a big, sweet, lumbering character who didn't seem too bright and didn't say much. In fact, when my first *UG* book came out, the subtitle was *America's Loveable Lug*.

Humphrey Bogart was another childhood hero of mine. He was the ultimate cool guy. Smart, tough, and clever, he could always see the way out of a problem. When I created a sidekick for UG, it seemed only natural that his best friend would be named Bogey. The two were inseparable. Bogey was a wise, savvy bird who usually perched on UG's head. Bogey looked out for UG, guided him, got him out of trouble, even did most of his thinking. Bogey may have been a bird, but he was no birdbrain. In many ways, like UG, Bogey was very much a part of me, albeit a hidden part that I wasn't overly in touch with yet.

And so it was in my late twenties that through UG and Bogey I gave physical form to two parts of my hidden character by literally drawing them from that secret place where our inner heroes live. Did I grasp this back then? No. What I understood came down to this: I knew I had talent, knew I had skills, knew I was good. But I grew up in my father's shadow, and rightfully so. Ziggy and Dad were the *real* superheroes. Yet millions of people were reading about UG and Bogey in the newspapers every day.

Talk about a prime case of not seeing the Batcave through the stalactites! I couldn't see the direct relationship between creator and creation, didn't grasp the role my inner self played in creating those characters who personified some of the best parts of my own. Who knows, maybe I was blinded by my own youthful ignorance and zeal, but I was *still* a Boy Wonder.

I'll be honest with you. I really wanted to be Batman. What guy wants to be Robin, the Boy Wonder, anyway? If Batman wasn't with him, it'd be a wonder the boy didn't get the guano kicked out of him on a daily basis. The suit was a joke. It looked like Peter Pan's Underoos. Batman had the cool suit. Batman had the gadgets. Hell, Batman probably *had* Catwoman! But did you ever see Robin get any of the cute chicks? And when it came to the Batmobile, Robin was never in the driver's seat. He was just a kid in a dorky outfit going along for the ride. He was there to make Batman look good. Robin was a wannabe superhero trapped in a boy's body.

UG was Robin to Ziggy's Batman. Yet like Robin to Batman, I never grew jealous of Dad; I felt only admiration, respect, and a kind of hero worship. I admire my father still, and as I look at that amazing magazine photograph of the four of us—Dad and me, Ziggy and UG—I realize it's the last time I can remember seeing Dad healthy, happy, and full of the passion, the exuberance he so generously shared and that naturally drew people to him.

Dad's health rapidly diminished thereafter.

So did my prospects as a grown-up Boy Wonder.

I had quit my job at the toy company and was focusing on *UG*. My sweet, lumbering, naive giant represented the last vestiges of childhood, along with the strengths and weaknesses that state of innocence harbors. Bogey, on the other hand, was no Robin. He personified the challenges and responsibilities of being an adult, and he stuck with me after UG officially went the way of the dodo.

My successful run with *UG*'s strip ran its course. Meanwhile, Susan became pregnant, so we moved out of Gotham City and in with her parents in Ohio to save money for our first home. In the process, I took some important lessons and realizations with me: UG was an overgrown, childlike character created for children by a young adult who had outgrown his own inner child. Adults called the shots in the real world, I learned, just as they did in the business of comics.

A very pivotal time in my life, I had reached an unexpected crossroads where the wonder of boyhood hit a dead end and the road I'd been traveling took a detour down a way too bumpy path.

Everything was about to change.

DOWNWARD . . .

THE HIGHWAY IS DANGEROUS. It's started to rain, so I proceed with caution. The wipers drone on, swiping away at the big wet drops and breaking the silence like a metronome metering out a steady beat as it patiently awaits some new tune to begin. The raindrops are coming harder, faster against my windshield, while the endless row of headlights continue from the opposing lane to assault my tired eyes.

Shifting from white to red, we pass each other, one by one, in the night: different points of light, different journeys, endlessly coming and going. And yet, the journey along this line of light is anything but pointless. *We* are the points of light, separate and finite, yet traveling together along this infinite circle of life. Anonymously we illuminate one another, mutually casting our shadows for one fleeting moment before passing on.

It seems a very natural balance takes place between the light and the dark, receding then surging forward like an ebb and flow, a tide. If light is faith and the substance of all things hoped for yet unseen, and darkness is the substance of all we blindly fear and never hope to see, what might shadow be? Perhaps there is some tenuous yet natural balance of awareness and understanding created from the contrast of that shadowy place between faith and fear where light and darkness meet. As if on cue, I sense Ziggy's comforting presence beside me. Like faith and fear, darkness and light, his character has emerged from such a balance of contrasts.

Ziggy comes from a world of imagination and ideas, only to be thrust into the realm of reality where each new day holds another custom-made ordeal for him to confront and overcome. Ziggy's obstacles are by design, even though from his perspective they may simply appear to occur by accident. Obstacles can slow us down, bring us to a screeching halt, or force us to change direction, making us feel that our journey is no longer moving forward as planned. We might find ourselves detoured into unknown territory, and yet every journey, like every life, has a specific purpose. Even if that purpose appears to happen by accident, that accident has purpose behind it.

As long as our roads are smooth and the traffic ahead is clear, we don't really notice the motion or the distance we're covering as we make our plans and set our courses toward reaching our goals as quickly as possible. It's only when we're forced to stop due to circumstances beyond our control or obstacles blocking our way that our perspective is suddenly forced to change and we become aware of just how much we've actually missed, ignored, and taken for granted.

As I continue to drive, I pass so many signs. However, I'm not aware of most of them. They don't really register unless they call to some want or need at the time—food, fuel, a direction to go.

Could it be that we miss something worthy of our attention because we're so involved with simply barreling down life's highway and only looking forward to something we think we need at the time?

I've just passed a sign: COLUMBUS: 75 MILES. I don't really know much about the city, maybe because it's never been my destination. Columbus is just *there*, a place I pass to get to where I'm going.

But wasn't Columbus also a guy who thought he knew exactly where he was going?

I can imagine Ziggy responding. *Yeah, until he got there and realized "there" wasn't where or what he thought it was going to be. And even if he didn't end up with what he was expecting, he did discover a whole new world instead!*

Occasionally, the communication between a creator and his character can lose a little something in translation, but there's nothing lost on me here.

Sometimes we're never more lost than when we think we're absolutely certain of where we're going. Just when we reach what we thought was our destination, we find ourselves in undiscovered country—a new world where nothing is what we expected it would be . . .

* * *

After *UG*, I was on unfamiliar ground yet close to home turf when Dad's health problems began. Ziggy originally came from Dad's passion within, and as that passion lessened in corresponding measure to his declining health, the necessity for me to pitch in was increasing. A gap had formed between Dad and his original character, and it was growing wider all the time. So I started helping Dad write *Ziggy*, do Ziggy gags, and this came easily to me. I did more writing until, eventually, I did practically all of it. Then I started inking Dad's pencil drawings, and before long, I was doing it all.

Having a true understanding of Ziggy was essential to my ability to take over for Dad. It's no less important today. I have to know how he experiences and perceives the world so he can directly communicate to his audience and evoke their personal understanding of and empathy with his message. Cartooning is a process, and everything begins with the *idea*—wherever that idea may be found or however it might find its way to the cartoonist. Because Ziggy's character is very simple and true, the messages and ideas he most effectively presents to others are generally those as simple and true as his own character.

As for a cartoon's physical creation, it's an orderly part of the process, unlike ideas, which can be elusive. The all-important idea is first lightly pencil drawn into Ziggy's 4×4-inch "Daily" panel-world. This allows me to get an initial sense of the cartoon's basic layout and composition. Once I have a rough pencil drawing on paper, I can step back and take a good look at what it is I intend to present to Ziggy's audience. This is the time for any mistakes to be made, any lessons to be learned from those mistakes, or any serendipitous opportunities to be discovered and incorporated into my work. The inking process now begins—the point of no return for the drawing. Committing to that indelible black line takes a leap of faith; my pen's ultimate path is a journey to bring the original idea to life. Only then do I erase my earlier pencil lines and present my finished cartoon to the world.

A significant difference exists between art and life when it comes to cartooning: in life, White-Out is not an option. Neither did I feel it was an option to bow out when Dad and Ziggy were counting on me. Ziggy needed to be cared for and looked after, and while I did this, I began to look after Dad in a parallel kind of way as his health dramatically suffered.

Though I was no longer doing *UG*, Bogey's character still lived in me, and one of the first things I did with Bogey was to introduce him to Ziggy's world through Josh, Ziggy's pet parrot. Josh was also the name of *our* pet parrot, a cantankerous green character I had purchased as a pet for Susan. But oddly enough, instead of bonding to Susan, Josh immediately adopted me as his new sidekick, choosing to spend all of his time perched on top of my shoulder.

Taking on *Ziggy* was the right thing to do, and I was the right person to do it because, beyond Dad, no one understood him better than me. To the best of my ability, I stayed in the background for many years. My reasoning was that to the rest of the world, Ziggy was Tom Wilson's character, and my father likewise needed that ongoing sense of public connection. This enabled not only the enterprise Dad had founded and built to continue, but also in many ways it allowed him to continue on as well. Too many people were depending upon Dad and Ziggy for me to bail out, but if I'm honest with myself, I think I depended upon both of them surviving more than anyone else. They were my heroes as a child, and while much has changed since then, that much never will.

As most of us do when we go through a major life transition, I look back on that time with mixed emotions. Although I had begun to "get Ziggy with it," I wasn't yet ready to face a rude awakening, and I didn't want the wonder my father had always created in me to die. Even if my Boy Wonder years as Robin were over . . .

. . . and the responsibilities that come with being Batman were mine instead.

When the security of following in Dad's footsteps and living in his shadow was gone, I found myself in a place as dark as any bat cave, stumbling and stepping in a lot of guano along the way. Without much warning, I had to run a business whose operation I'd observed from only a limited perspective. All of a sudden, every idea I had, every comic strip, every gag, every line I drew,

appeared before 75 million people every day for them to judge and, at least in my mind, to compare with each line and word my father had penned.

While most people never realized the transition had taken place, to me it felt very abrupt and not at all gradual. Fortunately, I eventually realized that I knew a lot more than I thought I knew. That, however, was small comfort because the entire situation was rife with discomfort, insecurity, and self-doubt. Often, taking over *Ziggy* felt like a major personal crisis, perhaps the first in my young life.

I was graced to have the support of a loving and understanding wife, as well as the continued support of our Ziggy & Friends vice president, Sue Dreher, who had inherited me after constantly keeping Dad organized for years. I still had a rudimentary self-confidence because I'd been doing a majority of the gag writing for *Ziggy* long before the actual transition took place, and found I had a genuine knack for the work, probably due to my understanding of and empathy for the character. Ziggy was, after all, my successful little brother. And spending most of my life getting to know him and watching him develop, I could feel comfortable writing the words Ziggy spoke and drawing the expressions he portrayed. I remain grateful for the extended period of time that enabled me to find the Ziggy part of myself from which I was able to create.

Yet, even then, I had to maintain a place behind the scenes on the public stage. In private I was doing the comic strip, but in public I receded into the shadows while Dad met the audience he so loved and needed. A lot of these appearances were signings for posters and prints at trade shows, and I would stand back, shoving the prints into envelopes after Dad had signed them for fans.

Eventually this would change. I remember one of the first times I publicly assumed the seat at an autograph signing, a couple of things happened. First, after ten minutes or so, it wasn't as scary as I thought it would be. Second, people didn't seem too surprised to see me signing when Dad was unable to attend.

Initially, though, I was really nervous because I wasn't accustomed to being observed by a crowd. I'd already drawn Ziggy a zillion times, but now I wasn't in the privacy of my house. I remember screwing up Ziggy's nose in a drawing. Artists at American Greetings called Ziggy's nose the Dead Man's Curve because it was such a challenge to get this curve between the eyes and nose right—it's in the profile where the round of the nose meets the bridge and curves up. The nose is almost something you feel rather than measure, and if you miss it, your Ziggy drawing is DOA. But if you hit it dead-on, you've got him nailed. Believe it or not, it can take years for even professional artists to perfect this miniscule thing with Zig's nose.

Anyway, I was doing this nose on a drawing for a little boy at a trade show and I screwed it up. But even though I messed up, the kids watching didn't seem to notice at all. I felt like apologizing and offering to do it again, but it was then I realized that I couldn't draw it wrong in their eyes. Because it came from the creator, they saw it as real and without flaw. I also realized that while I was very critical of myself, it was more important to them to see me do this drawing than for me to be upset because I didn't get it exactly right.

In the long run, this little "pootzelling" incident helped me relax and not be so hard on myself. Once again, I was reminded that the magic is much more important than the precision, and being true to one's own character is a far worthier goal than trying to live up to some real or imagined ideal we think others might expect.

While the art of the idea continued to be my personal passion, coupled with a deep and abiding romance with all things creative, some things in life not even a creator can predict, plan for, circumvent, or welcome as a part of the eternal process of change.

Yes, life predictably evolves, but it can still throw a Dead Man's Curve in our path even when we're behind the wheel of the Batmobile and racing toward the future at breakneck speed.

I think that's something we all can understand, especially after the unexpected happens on the road of life to forever alter the course of our journey.

My own hairpin turn came without warning. A sudden and unforeseen detour on what had been a pretty sweet ride—

Until Susan discovered a lump in her breast.

All of the mountains we had been preparing to conquer together for the better part of our married life were reduced to insignificant molehills overnight. Conquering that tiny lump, as well as the many that followed, became our greatest challenge and our most desperate crusade.

From the first day we discovered this archvillain called cancer had struck at the very heart of our life together, I witnessed the one constant in my life, my beautiful, sweet, gentle "Tweety Bird" become a hawk so fierce that General Patton himself would have saluted her. Susan went into battle with more strength and courage than any fictional superhero could possibly muster.

For my part, I became her second-in-command as every hope and dream we had previously held in life was put on hold to hold on to life itself. We went to war that day. That night she issued her very first order to me.

I will never forget the two of us standing in the shower together as I shaved her head, watching her long, beautiful hair fall in piles around our feet. I was crying. Her eyes were dry, and within them I saw the most powerful look of focused determination I think I will ever see. Susan opted for the strongest chemotherapy possible, and by taking her own hair, she determined to deny cancer its first victory.

Susan's hair was the kind you see in shampoo commercials, and her beauty . . . I can only describe it as timeless. But Susan's true beauty never came from the outside package, and that's something she always understood. Like her hair, her physical beauty was the first and only part of herself she willingly discarded. All that truly defined her came from within. It was from her soul that she drew her faith and her strength.

Though cancer had been found in one breast only, Susan opted for a radical double mastectomy, where *everything* is removed, including the lymph nodes leading up and into the arm from the breast. This was because her cancer had progressed beyond the third lymph node from her afflicted breast, which meant that in its journey, her cancer had found the on-ramp, racing from its place of creation onto a wide-open, four-lane highway throughout her entire body.

The hype is there before you see it, to prepare you for a horrible disfigurement. As a husband you don't really know what's going to happen until it actually does. At that first moment, you sense the apprehension in your wife's mind and you're probably not in much better shape because you've been told to anticipate this terrible physical vision.

It's not that way. You don't see the woman you love as any less a woman for lack of breasts, anymore than you suddenly find her repulsive. What you see is the woman you love, hurting and afraid, and the only thing that repulses you is the disease that brought this heart-wrenching agony upon her. The worst part is your own sense of how badly she must hurt from this, and the excruciating frustration you feel as a man from knowing that there's very little you can do to help take her pain away. When cancer is quietly going about its malignant mission, hidden beneath soft and familiar skin, you never get to see your enemy. But when breast cancer suddenly declares war, comes out in the open and shows itself in the tracks of sutures left behind, you suddenly realize that the woman you love more than anything in the world has not only come under attack, but has herself become the battleground. *This* makes you love her all the more and takes your love in a direction and to a height you never could have imagined possible.

I remember our first meeting with the plastic surgeon who gave Susan her breast implants. After our consultation, Susan and I stopped by the drugstore to pick up several popular men's magazines (*not* just for the articles) to get some ideas about what kind of new breasts we were going to get. Susan wasn't interested in having herself "supersized," and I agreed that the size she once had was just right for her and all that she'd ever need.

In truth, I think had we waited a while longer, she would have been fine with not having any implants, and that would have been fine with me, too. But I believe when things were still so fresh, replacing what had been taken away from her was something of a comfort for Susan and another way of fighting back to reclaim ground lost from our first major engagement with the enemy.

We also bought several wigs, and I remember attempting to put a happy face over an ugly reality by joking about how I would now be able to have a blonde one day and a redhead the next. The wigs fell by the wayside, almost as fast as my stupid jokes fell flat, and eventually Susan stopped wearing them altogether, choosing instead to give them away. She preferred to wear a scarf or nothing at all over her smooth, beautifully shaped little head.

Despite the radical mastectomy, we fought cancer for seven years after her initial diagnosis. We fought it through three remissions, a bone marrow transplant, daily blood transfusions, and constant infusions of some of the most toxic chemotherapy in existence. As Susan's cancer continued to grow and spread throughout her body, her faith seemed to grow exponentially throughout her spirit. Whatever faith I had came from Susan's strength.

My little Susan turned out to be the strongest person I have ever known. The life she lived inspired me throughout the life we created together and shared. She taught me that it's not what's on the *outside* that makes us who we are; it is who we are *inside* that truly defines us and grants us powers far beyond the physical. Our spirit is where our true strength resides, and it is our ark in times of crisis.

It was not until the final weeks of our twenty-two years together that I felt her strength begin to leave her small, cancer-ravaged body. She seemed to be loading on to her spiritual lifeboat and preparing to physically abandon ship. I remember her lying in that hospital bed, straining to raise her head from her pillow, and softly saying to me: "I think I have to go home soon, Tommy." We *both* knew what this meant, though I chose to ignore the implications her painfully conveyed words carried.

Shortly thereafter, in her room at a hospice, Susan slipped into a coma. Three days later, in the early morning, while I briefly left the room to search for comfort from a cup of coffee, Susan fought to hold her ground until she knew I had returned. When I came down the hall, the nurse rushed me into her room. It was then that I witnessed Susan making heaven wait as she lay suspended between it and Earth. In that moment, I joined her and kissed her gently as she opened her eyes one last time.

And as I held her, they closed again.

HEAVENWARD . . .

I JUST PASSED A sign for the Columbus city limits, which puts me only halfway home. After driving like a madman to make up for lost time, I've been crawling along for what seems like forever for the past few miles, and now the slow crawl has almost come to a dead stop.

Many of the cars look just like mine, and we're all heading in the same direction, progressing at the same slow speed. What strikes me is that with all these similarities, the individuals inside these vehicles are unique. Each of us is on a separate journey, yet we all share the same purpose in seeking some destination, and we all encounter the potholes and detours that unexpectedly present themselves while we're on our way.

Y'know, potholes and detours probably have a purpose, even when they jolt us, get us lost, and have us going in circles. Going around in circles tells us we're lost because we've missed another sign that was meant for us to see. Like the song says: "You don't know what you've got 'til it's gone," I suppose we don't know what we've missed 'til it's found. Sometimes, even though we may not like it, we may need to lose our way to find a better one.

I think we all have a tendency to do the same things repeatedly because that's where our habits and comfort zones come from. We get comfortable with routine and the feeling that going in circles is actually getting us somewhere. It's like the second hand on the clock that keeps ticking off the same numbers over and over again. The clock we're watching certainly knows what it's doing, and the second hand sure seems to know where it's going, but as we stand there thinking all is as it should be, precious time continues to pass us by.

I don't know how much precious time has passed for me to make this last mile, but what I do know is that I'm really tired of looking at that bumper sticker straight in front of me that says, "Whoever Dies with the Most Toys Wins!"

Yeah, right. Too bad there's no room to play with them in a cold, dark box underground.

The thought comes before I can stop it, and I'm suddenly feeling very ashamed for being so smug about something so deeply serious. No matter how expensive the coffin, *nothing* is luxurious about death, and it's rarely inclined to give us the courtesy of coming when we expect it.

Life, on the other hand, is our true luxury and—

WHOA!

. . . Flashing red lights just before the bridge.

Up ahead, I can see thousands of shards of splintered glass on the asphalt, sparkling red and white as they reflect the vehicle headlights and police strobes. Something thin and chromelike just passed under my tires.

It looks like they've cleared most of the larger pieces of metal out of the way, but I'm still hearing glass crunch beneath my wheels.

There's an ambulance here . . . puddles of something dark and wet near the side . . . oil, maybe . . . hopefully.

Okay, I see the rest of it. It's bad. Real bad.

There's a small blue car: wheels in the air, roof crushed to the ground. The gray car up ahead doesn't look any better. These cars aren't going anywhere, fast or slow, not ever again.

Based on what I see, I also have to believe that, in the case of at least one life, somebody is going somewhere completely unexpected tonight.

An old movie song unexpectedly enters my mind and I whisper to myself, *"Hello (New) World—Good-bye, Columbus!"*

I'm getting that heavy, sick feeling in the pit of my stomach and that cold, prickly sensation down the back of my neck. Strange how fear and loss seem to heighten our awareness.

Suddenly, everything seems suspended in time, moving in slow motion, even the hand of this officer waving us all forward. I'm looking at the wreckage. I have to look. We're *all* looking, we can't help it, and none of us likes to witness this awful thing we see.

I don't think we're really used to seeing the end of anything, at least not this dramatically, this finally. As I drive past, I hear the back door of the ambulance slam shut. It no longer seems to be in a hurry to go anywhere fast, either.

Through my rearview mirror, I see the flashing lights grow smaller and fainter behind me. Looking forward, I see the road is wide-open once again, beckoning me and the long line of red tail-lights ahead to keep going to where we all thought we were going before this terrible something happened.

Although the way ahead is now clear, I notice all of us are still moving a bit slower than we're able. Maybe it's due to where we've come from and what we've seen, reminding us that reaching our final destinations as quickly as possible isn't quite as important as actually getting there, or what can happen to us along the way . . .

* * *

Susan Shephard Wilson died in my arms on November 18. She was forty-four years old. Our two sons, Sam and Miles, were ten and thirteen, respectively.

After Susan went "home," I remember coming home from the hospice to Miles and Sam and having to tell them that their mother had passed away. It was one of the most difficult things I have ever had to do. I called them into the room, told them to sit down, and my mind went blank. I searched for some emotionally diplomatic or paternally soothing way to break the news, but there's just no good way to say "Mommy is dead."

They could see I was struggling to hold back my tears and came over to sit beside me, asking me what was wrong. All I could say was, "Mom passed away this morning, and now she's in heaven with God." In that moment I was aware of nothing beyond the expressions forming upon both their faces.

Sam, my youngest, had only known a small portion of his life with his mom as a completely healthy person. In a panicked gesture, he grabbed on to my arm, urgently pulling me up from the couch, and said, "C'mon Dad, let's go bowling." This surprised me at first, but I understood that, for him, it was a natural defense mechanism to do something he enjoyed to distract his thoughts from the new image of his mother lying cold and lifeless in a hospital bed, never to come home again.

His older brother, Miles, who for most of his formative years had known his mom as healthy and vibrant, immediately burst into tears, ran out of the room and up the stairs.

I remember how, in that moment, everything felt as if it were happening in slow motion: my son's tears, his frenzied ascent of the stairs, and the reverberating echo of his bedroom door slamming shut. Sam and I sat in frozen silence as we listened to the sound of things being thrown around overhead. As near as I can remember, Miles spent the rest of the day in his room crying. I'd periodically knock at his locked door, hearing only continued sobbing in response. Miles eventually told me to leave him alone, so I stayed as close to Sam as I could that day and as close to Miles as he would allow me to.

Their reactions brought into sharp focus that initially we each deal with extreme grief in a variety of ways—intense emotional outpourings, distraction, and denial among them. I remember thinking that my sons' pain must be unimaginable, even next to my own, but neither of their reactions could be an option for me. Too much needed to be done. Too much strength had already been lost through Susan, and our family was desperately in need of whatever strength I was still able to muster. Somebody had to keep the trains running on time, even though it now seemed that all tracks led nowhere.

Nothing about this present reality seemed real to me. I still couldn't wrap my mind around the fact that Susan was gone, that my boys were motherless, and that I had forever lost the very best part of my life. After so many years of witnessing Susan's painful struggle while I tried to help her battle cancer through chemo, bone marrow transplants, remissions, recurrences, and surgeries, I still didn't understand why I hadn't been better prepared to accept and deal with the outcome that apparently had seemed certain to everyone but me, her parents, and the boys.

In the months leading up to Susan's passing, numerous doctors and nurses had discreetly pulled me aside and advised me to start preparations for what they all believed to be the inevitable conclusion. I repeatedly and, I'm sorry to admit, often rudely rejected what those well-meaning medical folks had been attempting to prepare me for and to which I had refused to listen. Likewise, Susan's parents, the Reverend John and his gentle wife, Liz, had continued to maintain complete and unwavering faith that God would intervene and their beautiful little girl would be spared. And so, right up until Susan's final moment of life, we believed with all of our hearts and souls that God would give us a miracle and Susan would not be taken away from us.

Instead, the S.O.B. took her . . . and with her went my faith, along with whatever strength it seemed I still had left.

I remember sitting in the hospice parking lot in the car with the windows rolled up, crying, screaming at God and telling Him, "I know how much You love her and how much she loves You, but *we* only get a little bit of time with her here and *You* get her *forever*. How can You take her away from us now? Please, just bring her back." I offered God everything of any value I still possessed, and while I'm ashamed to admit it, I would have sold my soul to anyone or anything that could produce that particular miracle from their pocket. I remember being so angry at God when He took her, thinking how greedy He must be to want to keep her all to Himself when we needed her with us so much more. I cursed Him . . . and taking His silence for anger, I remember feeling immediately afraid and very, very guilty for my blasphemy.

In that moment I became more afraid of God than I had ever been in my life. I had just witnessed what He was so easily capable of doing: to devastate my family, and I knew that none of us could handle any more loss.

I had always believed Susan loved God as much, if not more, than she loved us. Or perhaps she loved us all in completely different ways. But it was Susan who had brought God into my life, and from seeing Him through her loving and trusting eyes, I had come to love and trust God as well. In my mind, Susan and God were as inseparable as I believed I was from her, and I had been happy with that arrangement because I believed He and I had a tacit understanding about sharing her. We had a deal, and it felt to me as if God had reneged.

My frustration turned to anger, which in turn led to more frustration . . . which again turned back to anger. God seemed silent to us, and I tried to bury my anger and keep it silent as well. Denial of God, however, was not a quid pro quo I could bring myself to initiate.

As hurt and betrayed as I felt over not receiving the miracle all of us had been expecting, were I now to deny the existence of God then, logically at least, I would also be denying the existence of heaven. Though logic, it seemed, no longer applied, I just could not bring myself to believe that Susan was not in heaven, in the arms of the God she loved so much in life. If I was to lose her in this life, how could I deny her life in the one that comes after?

Heaven, apparently, couldn't wait for our Susan, even though from what little I understood, God had all the time in the world on His hands! We, on the other hand, could wait no longer for somebody to save the day, and at this point I certainly wasn't counting on God to do it. From where I stood, He clearly had His own agenda that, for all intents and purposes, no longer included me or my children.

So much for prayers. So much for miracles. So much for saviors. But a savior was exactly what the three of us most needed, and I guess with my faith in ruins and the mercy of God an apparent fiction, it was only natural for me to reach back to the very fictitious characters I'd had faith in for so many years as a child. That's when I decided "This is a job for Superman!"

Superheroes, I had always observed, were never distracted from their missions or wasted time being angry; they just got things done. With our world and everyone around us doing a Krypton and going to pieces, I realized there was much here on planet Earth that needed to get done *immediately*.

Before I could begin putting my own house in order, I had to find a funeral home and a cemetery, and I had to order a plot, a casket, and a stone. I remember how nauseating it was to pick out a casket for the woman with whom you used to pick out wallpaper and curtains. I felt like I was being led through an automobile showroom with a high-pressure salesman. Add a set of radials on their top-of-the-line model, which resembled some kind of luxury import, and from the looks of the price tag it probably would be cheaper to be buried in a brand-new Lexus. In reality, the only necessary requirement of any of these heavily chromed and burnished high-performance beauties sitting on that showroom floor was that they managed to do zero-to-six-feet-under in less than sixty seconds.

Still, I ended up getting her the most beautiful casket they had, knowing full well that Susan would have wanted something very simple. Guilt does strange things to you; it can make you act in ways you normally wouldn't. Grief takes that to an entirely different level.

Ultimately, I ended up sinking well over half of our life savings into Susan's funeral, burial, and monument. She had worked tirelessly to help support us while I finished school, and continued to work until we started having children. For more than twenty years, Susan and I had managed to set a little aside each year, so that one day we would be able to buy a home in Hilton Head, where we would retire. We'd spent several summer vacations there with her parents, and she had always found it to be beautiful and peaceful. Susan always loved the ocean and I had always loved Susan, so that was our plan: to grow old together, spending our remaining golden years by the sea, surrounded by peace, comfort, and beauty.

Now with Susan in heaven and Hilton Head paradise lost, I'd be damned if she wasn't going to take along with her part of what she'd scrimped and struggled to save for our future together. After all, our golden years spent on the beach, leaving side-by-side sets of footprints in the sand, had all been deep-sixed as well.

I kept trying to bury my anger over what I felt had been a divinely gross miscarriage of justice, but it resurfaced again and again throughout the process of making the arrangements for Susan's final resting place.

Eventually I found myself in an office with the tombstone sales-person, and she asked me what I would like to have inscribed on the headstone. The woman had produced a lovely catalog, replete with a large assortment of very popular and personal endearments and epithets. As I scanned the endless glossy pages of marble Hall-markers, I zoned out in much the same way I do when selecting birthday cards in the greeting card aisle at the grocery.

My mind drifted back to that time when Susan and I were just married and had moved to Boston. She had taken a job as a pack-age designer at a plastic bag plant outside of the city. I hated that place because every time I went in to visit her, the atmosphere was always thick with the haze of PVC fumes from the plastic bags they manufactured on-site. Whether or not that had any-thing to do with her illness years later, I'm left still guessing.

But I do remember her coming home one day, absolutely ecstatic, excited to tell me something that had happened at work. Of course I assumed she'd just received a raise or promotion or something along those lines because she was radiant with joy. Instead, she told me that when she had taken a break for lunch and was alone, she actually heard God's voice speaking to her.

Well, naturally my first question was: What did He say? I sup-pose I was expecting some earthshaking revelation or perhaps even an eleventh commandment, but instead she just smiled and told me, "He said to me, *'You refresh Me with your love.'*"

So, to the convincingly sympathetic tombstone saleslady, I quoted the words of God Himself. And with a few strokes of her pen, our terms of endearment were finally concluded, and once again, the words of the Almighty became permanently etched in stone.

Apparently, not only had God managed to spirit away from us our future, He even managed to reach back from our past to get in the last word.

Or so I thought.

INWARD . . .

BACK ON I-71, I'm thinking that I've always believed laughter is good for the soul, and sometimes you just have to laugh to keep from crying. But I've gotta tell ya, it will be no laughing matter if I don't do something quick about the blinking red light on my gas gauge. While I can run on coffee, or even on empty as I often do, the old Batmobile is now practically running on fumes. I feel my anxiety rise as I look in earnest for another exit. Any exit will do, just somewhere I can pull over, refresh myself, and refill my tank. The low rumble of my stomach reminds me that I have two tanks that need filling, and from over the dark horizon I see the first light of promise from a new sign rise, just when I need it the most.

Then the signs appear and gather, hovering on high like a band of luminous and bloated angels, each shilling their own particular brand of high-cholesterol manna along the highway to hamburger heaven. Again, it looks like we have the usual suspects here: fast-food joints, gas stations, and convenience stores, all conveniently combined,

so now we can eat *and* get gas at the same time and place!

Arriving on a wing and a prayer with an empty tank of fossil fumes, I pull into the nearest all-in-one superstation. After pumping up, I head straight to the "head," then bound to the fast-food restaurant a few steps away. There, I stand transfixed before the harvest gold Formica altar, perusing a menu of epic proportions. Temptations abound. I can't decide whether to Supersize my Happy Meal, Happysize my Super Meal, or Valuesize my Super-Happy Meal . . . I buy gum and nuts.

I remember a time not too long ago when no one ever asked if we wanted anything supersized; they assumed, just as we did, that what was received was all that one really needed. Fact is, if you're full, you're full . . . and when you're feeling empty deep down inside, you can get free refills until your cup runneth over, or eat Happy Meals till you puke, and still not be fulfilled.

Regardless of preservatives, maybe we've become spoiled by our expectations that we have the option of making anything "Super" in a very quick and convenient way. Maybe this plays to our desire to supersize *everything* in life, whether we need it or not. But the truth is that bigger and faster aren't always better (although it's never been easier to get bigger faster!). And like their sandwich-variety counterparts, our heroes or our miracles may not always appear larger than life or arrive faster than a speeding bullet. More often than not, the answers to our prayers arrive unexpectedly and turn out to be what we *need*, not always what we *want*.

Immediately Ziggy comes to mind as a perfect example of this. He's anything but super in size or shape, but by showing up for work each morning and joining us in the funny pages for coffee and another serving of life's daily grind, Ziggy has become a hero of sorts to many. He speaks directly to all the other unsung every-day heroes dealing with their own everyday challenges in their everyday ways, and I believe that's why he connects on such a human, yet heroic, level. I can honestly say that Ziggy has always been there for me, and I know he always will be.

Somewhat more refreshed, I'm shooting back onto the highway, leaving my doubts, anxiety, appetite, and good chunk of change on the side of the road. The highway before me is wide-open, so I set the cruise control, sit back, and get comfortable. With no obstacles in sight, I'm steering into the darkness, confident that I know exactly what lies ahead and just when I'll get there, albeit later than I initially expected.

Then again, the most unexpected things can happen when we're on cruise control within our comfort zones, and it's usually what we don't see coming that can hit us hardest, leave us scrambling to find our balance and trying to make sense out of what, at the time, doesn't seem to make any sense at all. And while it may seem to have no purpose, much less any heavenly kindness or human justice, in a really bad situation, an opportunity can still be found to *do* something good, *find* something good in even the most tragic of situations.

It seems to me it's then when real miracles unexpectedly appear and everyday heroes emerge, when we can call out the hero inside to help ourselves, help others, and overcome the most daunting of odds. If life is like a box of chocolates, then we *all* are in this box together. And while you never know what you're gonna get in life, from the chocolate's point of view, you never know who's gonna get you . . . or how you're going to change the lives of those who gotcha.

Sometimes we need to be knocked out of the chocolate box to look from the outside in, to see beyond the comfy compartment surrounding us. Since this usually means getting knocked out of our comfort zones and having to deal with life's challenges as well, we don't like that. And we don't have to. But I do believe there has to be a way to successfully incorporate change into our natural desire for order, simply by learning to expect the unexpected . . .

* * *

Shortly after Susan's passing, I received an unexpected package from a woman who hardly knew me. The note she attached said that she'd been walking through a store when she suddenly heard God tell her, *Buy this journal for Tom Wilson.*

Now at that point, God and I were not exactly on speaking terms. Yet apparently He still had something to say, and I remember thinking He didn't even have the guts to tell me Himself.

Frankly, I never anticipated doing any journaling, even if it was a lovely gesture from this kind woman. But as a gift from God Almighty, it was a far cry from the gift we'd all prayed for so faithfully to receive, and to be honest, my first inclination was to tell

God where to shove it. It was kind of a "My Family Went Through Hell . . . And All I Got Was This Lousy T-Shirt" moment.

Ultimately, I ended up shoving the journal into a nearby drawer instead of where I felt it really belonged.

I've heard it said that the opposite of love is indifference not anger, even if it's anger that's unexpressed. At the time I was anything other than indifferent about God. I truly felt entitled to be angry and hurt by what appeared to be His indifference to me.

I kept trying to figure out *why*. Why do these things happen? How could such a gentle soul with so much faith and love for God be subjected to so much pain and misery within her short life? And how could such a God completely ignore the prayers

and the pleadings of those who loved that gentle soul so much? I remember at one point thinking shit happens, but with so much shit raining down upon our family and our lives, only the largest asshole in the universe could be responsible.

I know how stupid this sounds. I know how childish my thoughts and behavior were at the time, but I felt justified and hurt. It was only later that I realized that while God does hear our prayers, He doesn't always answer them in the ways we expect.

About a month later, don't ask me why, I found myself pulling the journal from the drawer. Embossed footprints run along the front cover, with the title *Footprints* and the famous poem about a person walking with God on a beach. At the lowest points in this person's life the two sets of footprints dwindle to one, and the seeker asks the Lord why He deserted him in his greatest times of need. God explains that when only one set of footprints appear, "it was then that I carried you." I wasn't really sure why I opened that journal and began to write. Maybe I wasn't able to express myself any other way. Or perhaps I desperately needed to resolve the paradox of how Susan could be in the arms of a loving God when that same God seemed either indifferent to our prayers or simply nonexistent.

Writing, I quickly discovered, became a way for me to gain a larger perspective on feelings and issues that were far too close for comfort within my bewildered thoughts. And since it felt like no one was listening, writing gave me a method to speak to myself and let my thoughts unfold as they arrived.

Before long, much within me began to flow out and onto those pages, and after careful review, what flowed back was the genesis of a new understanding.

At some point, though I never heard His actual voice, I began to wonder if the words appearing miraculously before me were perhaps coming from God Himself as a form of comfort and a sign that He does indeed listen and, in fact, knows me well enough, loves me enough to forgive me for any thoughts I might feel ashamed about having.

Another voice of comfort came to me in the form of a very familiar friend named Ziggy. I remembered back to those days long ago at Big Boy when a little boy and his larger-than-life father spent their mornings playing SAVE ZIGGY! And there I was, decades later, fully grasping the lesson my father had taught me: the first and easiest solution to any dire crisis situation may not necessarily be the best. Though it didn't happen right away, somewhere down the line Ziggy and my father reached up from that placemat not only to help save Tom, but Tom's faith as well.

Thus began a long yet miraculous process of digging deeper to find answers to questions that, so long ago in that restaurant, a young boy never thought he'd have to ask. Not only would my journey to come prove to be a case of life imitating art, a reversal of our SAVE ZIGGY! game, but a very real lesson that when bad things happen, while we may not understand why at the time, there's always a purpose for the hard challenges we face.

A month after Susan died, I took the first steps on a very zigzagging path through this So-Journaling of discovery and new understanding.

Journal Entry
December 14

It's been almost a month since Susan's passing. I find myself thinking of her constantly. The memories of Susan in pain and fear are fading, only to be supplanted by images of our youth together, and though they seemed insignificant then, those memories have now become so precious. I miss her so much.

What am I without true love in my life? Is what I'm to become even important without it?

I like to think that time is an earthly thing, important only to those who dwell here and that it has no meaning in heaven. I like to think I'm already there with Susan, where we will have many more lifetimes together to come.

I feel Susan with me everywhere I go. She's young and healthy again and so comforting. I feel her most when I'm sad and her presence lifts my spirits somehow. When I'm watching Sam play basketball, I know she's there beside me in the stands, watching him, too. When I'm hearing of Miles's new interest in girls, I know she's listening as well. What a pity she couldn't be here on earth, alive, to share the pleasure of watching these two wonderful sons of ours mature.

This Christmas will be hard without her here on earth. I realize now more than ever how much I drew from her seemingly unlimited strength.

The friendships and loves we accumulate are the truest measure of progression we have through this life. Love is so much more than a word or the human feelings it elicits. It's a way of life we create together, and living is the journey we travel, marked along the way with milestones of hellos, and sadly, good-byes.

But even good-byes are only temporary, and in the end, not really good-byes, since lifetimes are immeasurably small portions of life itself.

December 18

I'm sitting in our living room. It's Sunday morning, snow is softly falling outside, and the boys are still upstairs sleeping.

I've got Christmas music on the stereo as I watch our new lil' train go 'round the beautiful Christmas tree. Our little dog, Molly, has just come over to comfort me by chewing her rawhide bone on the tops of my bare feet in a very painful way. She doesn't know what it means when I've been crying uncontrollably, yet somehow she knows I need to be comforted, or what passes for comforting in a sweet, loving English bulldog's mind.

It's obvious what's missing in this idyllic picture—so obvious. The most upsetting aspect of it is that no matter what I do, I'll never be able to put this picture right. Susan is gone. She won't be coming back for the rest of my life.

I know how blessed I am to have had a great love in my life. I've seen how rare a thing it can be. With that blessing comes a cruel appendage. I live completely in a new reality now. The intoxicating dream of sharing a lifetime together has been slapped out of me by recent events.

I've awakened to the hangover of a reality without my wonderful Susan ever to be in my life again.

I don't remember much about the holidays that year, except I think we had a Thanksgiving bird, a Christmas plane, and tickets to take us *Up, Up and Away!* to the most expensive vacation I could possibly afford. While there I scribbled in my journal, "The boys and I went to the Bahamas and found some quality

time together, beauty, fun, peace, and ourselves many thousands of dollars poorer."

The truth is money can't buy happiness anymore than two weeks at a Caribbean resort can buy a respite from grief.

Oddly, though, while Susan was constantly in my thoughts, I didn't seem to be grieving. When we arrived home, my emotions seemed to come to a dead stop and completely close down. Although I'd always been a disorganized person, I became the most efficient, orderly man I ever knew, deciding that what my life and my children needed most was structure and order, because, remember *"This was a job for Superman,"* definitely *not* Clark Kent. As for all of the Kryptonite raining down upon me, inside and out, I ignored its existence. Nothing could touch me—not even death.

People wondered why I wasn't grieving. I told myself that I simply didn't have time, when in truth I didn't *want* to grieve. Grief seemed like acceptance that this loss was real and permanent.

I didn't realize it then, but I was struggling to build a lean-to in the eye of a hurricane. I look back on that time and can't believe I had these abilities within me. Hasn't that happened to all of us? Can't we all look back to a low point in our lives, some situation we'd never want to revisit, and be amazed at what we were capable of doing when the only other alternative was to simply lie down, give up, and be blown away?

Anyway, in a single bound I went from burying Susan to going on a vacation, to sitting in the bleachers at every game while Sam played basketball, and making sure Miles got his homework finished. I met my *Ziggy* deadlines. Our house was clean and our meals microwaved to perfection. I started working out regularly to deal with the stress, and because it gave me a sense of control over my body, I got into the best physical shape I'd been in since my swim team years.

I decided that I had to begin rebuilding my life faster than a speeding bullet, to try to forget the past and even to start dating again. It didn't matter that I had no idea what the hell I was doing in the dating world after being married to my better half for the better half of my life.

The way this happened was more accidental than deliberate. Actually, it was Susan's sister who set me up to meet a certain someone at a Valentine's party. There I met a woman whom I'll call "Lois."

It had been so long since I'd felt an attraction to any woman besides Susan, and Lois was a lane I hadn't intended to travel, but I found her so intriguing and mysterious that my attraction to her was both immediate and intense. I was besieged with guilt and had even written in my journal earlier how I was sure that

Susan wouldn't like another woman coming into our lives and home. I couldn't imagine inviting another one in, especially one who could not be more different from Susan.

Even so, that didn't stop me from doing something that was completely out of character for me, which was to send Lois a note after the party, telling her how much I enjoyed meeting her. I was completely unprepared for her mailed response, a very funny card suggesting that I call and we get to know each other better.

The day I received her card, I wrote in my journal:

I'm a total basket case now. I've thought about Lois a great deal this past week. WHY? I guess I should call her and arrange a date, but honestly I'm afraid I'm not going to live up to her expectations. I feel like a teenager again. Is that bad? I'm beginning to understand that I need to meet people. They were never as important to me before because Susan fulfilled my social needs. Susan and I were a single unit. And now with her gone it's like I need to discover an entirely new part of myself.

I haven't a clue about that part: interests, capabilities, or personality. I think it may have some interesting aspects to it, and I'm actually anticipating each new discovery. I know the best thing to do is just relax and be myself; the trouble, of course, is I don't know who myself is. How am I going to behave on a date in the presence of another woman? Will I be a fool? Will she sense my nervousness and still be nice enough to look behind it? Will I even be nervous? It's only been 25 years since I dated. I suppose I should release this all to the fates and relax, but I have neither a clue nor a chance when it comes to relaxing. First dates are scary enough for those who are not in my current position. Well, let's see what I'm made of.

As it turned out, that first date went so well that Lois and I soon became involved, and I actually imagined myself falling madly in love again. My mother would later liken it to the story of Lysander in Shakespeare's *A Midsummer Night's Dream*, who had a spell put upon him to fall into a deep sleep only to fall hopelessly in love with the first woman he met upon awakening.

I continued, of course, to grapple with my new and terrible guilt for being unfaithful to Susan, even though she was gone and wasn't coming back. That guilt was compounded, and my new relationship increasingly complicated, because Lois didn't have children of her own and couldn't understand why Sam would call me half a dozen times during a dinner date. She resented the intrusion, and I found myself caught in the middle between my twin identities of Single Man and Single Dad.

In addition to that, I had found another diversion in trying to find "The New Me." Lois moved freely in the upper echelons of an avant-garde, contemporary art circle, which, for some reason, welcomed me with open arms. I'm sure that because Lois was something of their reigning Queen of Bohemia, and I was her current consort, it helped a great deal as far as their accepting me into their world.

For my part, I really liked this crowd. They were intelligent, eclectic, and appeared well adapted to and adept at bending chaos to their creative wills—exactly what I was struggling to learn myself. So by night I donned my black T-shirt and slacks and played the role of high-profile celebrity/tortured artist among the artistic underworld. And by day, I was back in my minivan, driving kids to Little League practice and helping assemble Styrofoam models of the Colosseum for school history projects.

What I didn't realize was that I had my alter egos all screwed up. Celebrity-playboy Bruce Wayne and Superman just didn't go together, especially when in reality I had much more in common with Clark Kent than I wanted to admit.

I desperately wanted it to work with Lois and the boys, and I was beginning to think that they needed a woman in the house more than I did. I wondered if I was really just trying to put my family back together again by using this other woman, the first one to come along, or if I was distracting myself from deeper issues and unfairly trying to fit someone else into a role for which she simply was not suited.

Meanwhile, Miles began to act out, and I remember a terrible argument we had when he threatened to behave badly toward Lois if I didn't let him use the computer I had taken away as a disciplinary measure for being disrespectful and challenging my authority the night before. He no doubt saw me in a vulnerable situation and tried to take advantage, but I had to show him I was still strong, so I put him in his place. He backed down, but Sam stood up for him. I had to let them both know that behind my patient and controlled role of running the family lay the responsibility of parenting and that I would *not* be blackmailed by my children.

As for Lois, she had her own strong opinions about how I was raising my kids. So the tug-of-war ensued and I was the rope. It was as if everyone was claiming their turf, and at this point it was a no-win situation for me. I decided I had to wait it out, get to a point where I lasted longer than these opposing forces, and come to some new understanding of the process that was occurring so I could better determine the best way to go.

One of the few times I brought Lois into my home, the situation became unbearable. The children were actively misbehaving when I needed them to behave and make her feel welcome.

I needed that trade-off from them so she would not be overly critical of the behavior my children were exhibiting to take advantage of the awkward situation in which I had placed myself. Ultimately, that night ended with Lois saying that if she'd had children, they would have turned out much better than mine. Again I held my anger. That first night together in Susan's and my house, and in Susan's and my bed, Lois and I went to sleep in cold silence.

The following morning I awoke with Lois beside me, sitting up in bed, a stricken expression on her face. When I asked what was wrong, she told me she had not slept most of the night because she had woken up in the middle of it to find a young girl standing at the foot of our bed, staring at her angrily. She said this girl told her that she should not talk about Miles and Sam this way, that they were terrific children. Lois then apologized to me and said she was wrong for saying what she had about my kids.

I asked her to describe the image she'd seen at the foot of the bed. She said the girl was about nine or ten years old, wearing a yellow dress, with a pageboy haircut. The girl she described was identical to a picture Susan's parents have of her as a little girl, with that same dress and haircut.

Even Susan apparently felt the need to respond to my lack of expressing emotion and righteous indignation. It also made me realize that no matter how much I may have wanted to put things right by reconstructing a traditional family, Lois would never be the one to do this with, and I had been unfair to both her and the

boys by asking them to accept my imagined scenario.

I wasn't immediately willing to accept the inevitable yet again, but all those plates on sticks I'd been spinning like crazy to maintain some semblance of balance in our lives were beginning to wobble.

WAYWARD . . .

I'M STILL CRUISING along I-71 with no flashing red strobe lights, blinking gas lights, or rain in sight. What is too plainly in sight is a flat, empty sea of farmland directly ahead. Not empty enough, however, given the huge homemade sign, obviously planted with purpose in some farmer's field, coming into view through my bug-splattered windshield. Getting closer, I can make out the giant letters scrawled across the surface of this thirty-foot-high sign:

IF YOU DIED TODAY,
WHERE WOULD YOU SPEND *ETERNITY*?

Passing over to the other side, I glimpse a list counting down the top five commandments of the Creator's Big Ten.

Another hundred yards later, facing the highway from behind barbed wire, yet more light reading for the happy motorist:

HELL IS REAL!

I need a sign to tell me that? It's no surprising revelation that the backside hosts the final installment of commandments VI to X.

As I drive on, putting these signs behind me, I'm not thinking about hell, home, or my kids, not even about getting somewhere fast and all in one piece. What I'm thinking about now is eternity . . . and that I'm feeling old . . . and tired. With miles to go before I sleep, this particularly lonesome stretch of highway is beginning to take its toll. I've seen much more than I ever planned on seeing—literally and figuratively—taken more detours than I ever planned to take, and as for signs? Well, I've been led by more of those than I could follow in a lifetime.

What I've noticed about signs is that even if they're not etched in stone, they're still a lot like miracles. They're everywhere, but we only really notice them when we need something—and that's when the signs or miracles we're searching for seem to make themselves scarce. There are plenty of signs we choose to ignore, while others refuse to grant us that luxury. Unfortunately, some signs seem much better at reading us than we are at reading ourselves. But what I think actually matters most about signs is not necessarily what they say, but how they manage to affect us.

Hell is real! No shit.

Death as Art/Roadside Kitsch.

I swear, I mean no offense by my comments. In fact, the Ten Commandments have always commanded my respect, and I'm a big fan of Moses. After all, I've studied superheroes religiously most of my life, and in many ways, when you think about it, Moses was the original Superman. In the beginning, both Superman and Moses set sail on their life journeys over waves of crises.

Each was launched upon a desperate voyage of survival at birth; two innocent-looking anomalies carried along in a fragile vessel by the currents of heaven and earth. Salvaged by the hands of fate, they began a new life that raised them to full stature, imbuing them both with great powers.

At some point, however, the merged paths traveled by Superman and Moses clearly appear to diverge. While Superman's path led him on a journey in search of his own humanity, Moses' path took him to much higher ground; his became an exodus toward the divine.

From everything I've read, Moses was outstanding in the field of translating *big* signs from the Creator, so I can't help but wonder what he might have thought of those giant signs standing out in the field that I've just passed.

Heaven only knows the answer to that one, and while I'm by no means a religious scholar, I do believe that there were signs along Moses' exodus journey, leading him along a hero's path, that we can learn from.

In my abbreviated version of *The Exodus*, Moses frees God's people from bondage in Egypt and eventually pulls the children of Israel over for a little rest stop in the shadow of Mount Sinai, where he hikes to the top for some guidance.

Now I'll have to admit that I've struggled to understand the point of making Moses climb all the way to the top of a mountain only to send him back down again while carrying two heavy stone tablets.

The point, I've decided, is that Moses' mountain is a good indi-cator of just how precarious and difficult our own uphill journey can be to tread as we try to find our purpose and not let self-doubt or critics or obstacles overcome the realization of whatever that specific purpose in life might be. Yet, once we finally stumble upon our true purpose, purpose *creates* our path, and once com-mitted to that path there "ain't no mountain high enough, ain't no valley low enough," or river too wide to keep us from what we are compelled to do.

In navigating our way from the desert to our own Promised Land, might it be possible to come out better on the other end than before setting out on a journey we never anticipated, and certainly never would have asked for? That's quite a challenge, but certainly a worthy one to undertake.

As for the people Moses led and the challenges they faced, the next generation emerges from the desert to finally reach their Promised Land. Although it's minus Moses when they get there, a magnificent container, the ark of the covenant, arrives along with them.

The Old Testament says that the ark, which housed the Ten Commandments, emanated a living energy of unfathomable power and doubled as a two-way communicator between God and His people. To make a long story short, the ark—containing the Creator's instructions for us—eventually becomes lost, buried somewhere beneath the drifting sands of time.

Regardless of one's religious beliefs, this is still a fascinating story. Many believe it all to be literally true, and I won't disagree with them, but who is to say that this story couldn't *also* be true in a figurative sense?

Suppose our true life journey is *our* individual exodus out of self-inflicted bondage to ourselves, and due to our own ignorance or foibles, we have cursed ourselves to forty years of wilderness wandering (read: midlife crisis) until some personal epiphany sets us back on our original path.

It does seem to be part of the human condition that the less we have of anything, the more precious to us it becomes. This is never more apparent than when we look back upon our life in its entirety as we grow older. Maybe that's why, when middle age hits, a lot of us suddenly find ourselves asking these venerable questions: Where is my life going? What should I have done differently with it? What have I been missing? What haven't I achieved?

These are all very good questions, and the sooner we ask them, the better, because it gives us that much more time to act upon the answers. Of course, to reveal some answers may require deep, internal digging. We may even feel like archaeologists, trying to uncover the clues from our past that we wish we'd had while going through the motions of living, but never really living life the way we envisioned while we were young.

Like the ark and the Ten Commandments it contained, the idea that God's gift of our life purpose arrives with its own instruction book makes sense to me. Unfortunately, many of us consider our books to be like an empty journal, full of blank pages waiting to be filled up and written to make us feel more presentable to those we consider, or would like to consider, our peers. Because of our insecurities, we too often judge ourselves guilty of imperfection and in so doing give our power away to others by essentially allowing them to become our personal editors.

The Old Testament chronicles Moses' entire life story, from the beginning of his journey down the Nile to the end of his epic forty-year dash to the Promised Land. Likewise, *our* life stories contain page after page of the greatest in drama, comedy, love, tragedy, and mystery, which continues to turn with unexpected twists from the first breath life gives us to the last gasp death takes.

In thinking back to those signs in the farmer's field that set me off on this little digression, I find myself wondering why they make me feel so angry. What is it about them that could affect me so deeply, that could elicit such a gut-deep, resentful response?

I'm digging inside for an answer, and the best explanation I can come up with is that it reminds me a bit too much of that time in my past when I was wandering around my own personal desert with no exodus for me and my family in sight. I needed direction, some sign to tell me which way to go. At the same time, I didn't want anyone getting in my face, the way those Ten Commandment signs do, imposing their own judgments on me, even if my judgments were less than sterling, given the unbalanced state of mind I was in.

It's difficult to reflect on that time without cringing. Not only had the plates begun to wobble, my personal editors were starting to step in . . . and I let them.

* * *

Family had always been a large part of what defined me. I'd come to a place in my life where I realized that above all else I needed to be cognizant of how important family and friends were while continuing to discover just who I was without Susan. Although I could feel myself losing emotional ground and sensed my defenses couldn't continue to withstand the increasing pressure, I instinctively knew that life was a great balance of things, and balance was the most important skill I needed to master.

Knowing and doing, of course, aren't the same things, and my

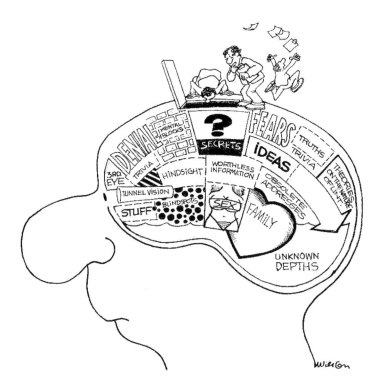

personal balance became further compromised when my father suffered a major stroke somewhere in this time frame. Although they never divorced, my parents had amicably parted ways, so the duty of overseeing Dad's health care fell to me, which continues to this day. I shouldered this responsibility then, as I do now, with the knowledge that I've been given an opportunity to return the love my father gave me as a parent, only with our roles now reversed.

What I learned in short measure, however, was that the stress in my life was beginning to overwhelm me, and I didn't like the unbalanced and confused shell of a person to which I felt I was becoming reduced. I picked up smoking. I felt lost, lethargic, confused, completely indecisive, relying on others to tell me which way to go because it seemed I could no longer trust my decisions, thoughts, or understandings. I was so lost it was beginning to feel more and more that nobody was home inside.

Still, I continued to journal, because it was the closest thing I could grab on to and take some solace from when everything else in my life seemed more and more out of control.

Journal Entry
August . . . ?

I was resting within the peaceful eye of a hurricane for most of my marriage to Susan. Peace, happiness, and joy enveloped us until slowly and unknowingly we drifted toward the outer boundary of that calm place and neared the event horizon.

We were caught up in the current the day we discovered Susan's cancer, and each day for more than seven years the current pulled us farther from the peace of the eye and into rougher elements. This eye closed for me the day Susan's closed forever.

The hurricane is relentlessly battering my ship, and use of my compass, now spinning wildly out of control, has become pointless . . . I am the captain of a ghost ship with tattered sails and a damaged rudder. I've lost my True North and no longer have any star to steer by.

For the first time in my life, going down with my ship has become a very real possibility, and I fear losing my grip on the wheel, being swept overboard, and carried away. As I desperately search for some support to help me hold on, I find only broken railings and slippery footing.

I know that while the eye is now beyond my sight, it watches my progress still. This storm is a heartless killer, and in the graveyard beneath its waves rest the skeletons of many more majestic ships, commanded by far more experienced captains.

In the depths below, the dead calm of the eye is eternal. But here at the helm, the lashing sting of wind and wave on my face, and the queasy turmoil in my mind and body, tells me that while I'm at the mercy of the elements, I'm still alive and full of fight. This realization stirs me and fixes my resolve to ride the storm out.

So there you have it, a general idea of where my head was at in this particular moment. Just about that same time, my relationship with Lois became so on-again off-again it seemed to change by the day—not too surprising given all of this internal and external mayhem that was doing a supernova in the black hole that was becoming my so-called life.

Then suddenly, and I mean *suddenly*, without warning, that's when the depression hit . . . and not just your middle-of-the-road, standardized definition of depression. This was an odd kind of depression, a pervasive malaise that defied definition, presenting itself in an unanticipated, subtle, and insidious way.

In less than a New York minute, my carefully orchestrated, albeit fragile, structure, the foundation of order I'd rebuilt our house upon, disappeared. *Poof!* Vanished overnight. The shelter that I'd sought refuge within was only a house of cards, and once it could no longer hold up beneath all that was expected of it, nothing and no one was left to put it back together again. Even order no longer granted safe harbor, and my kids, my dad, all I had left of my family were still counting on me to give them at least that much. At that point it appeared Superman had succumbed to all the Kryptonite around him, even though his help was needed more than ever.

I hired a nanny out of desperation to keep the kids fed and looked after. I felt responsible and guilty for everything. I was trying, doing my best, but I knew I was still coming up short. I needed to be firmer with the boys, less permissive. Since I was acting as two parents, I felt I had to be the one to assert authority. We could be the Three Amigos no more (or so Lois and others had convinced me, which wasn't difficult because I didn't trust my own judgment).

I still clung to a shred of hope that my relationship with Lois would work, even though clearly it would not. Lois expressed her belief that whatever I was going through was getting worse and I was becoming emotionally stunted, even referring to me as "handicapped." I told her that I never asked for this thing to be put upon me, that I was doing everything I could. I told her that this was not "the real me," that it felt like an alien presence in my life, which was new, akin to a vicious virus that had been unasked for and was unwelcome. This malaise was a thing of which I wished to rid myself, and with time and patience, I *would* eliminate it from my life because it was anything but a permanent aspect of my personality. I don't know who I was trying to convince more, Lois or myself.

I do know that Lois tried but she didn't understand. I can't completely blame her. It is so hard for anyone who hasn't lost a beloved spouse to understand the process of grieving a soul mate.

The boys' happiness with any woman I was seriously involved with was very important to me. I knew that engaging in a hedonistic, escapist romance was selfish and wrong, and my prime directive had to be to care for my boys first and foremost, putting their needs above all others, especially my own.

So, after approximately six months, I ended a relationship that probably should never have been. In retrospect, I realize I had begun to date not only far too early, but for all the wrong reasons. Dating was a big thing and I shouldn't have gone anywhere near a woman when I did. All I can guess is that besides going through a major identity crisis minus Susan, I fell into the same statistical trap a lot of recently widowed men do, hoping a woman would come along and we could resume a normal family life again.

It's lucky for Lois that we called things off. I rapidly began to spiral downward even as I yearned for balance, order, and simplicity. While I had managed to somehow convince myself that where Susan was concerned, "life after death" was an indisputable fact, in my own case, I wasn't so sure. I still had a lot of unexpressed anger, but my passion had left me. My thoughts and feelings had become an internal mass of confused ideas and contradictory actions.

I felt truly lonely and yet I was never alone. I needed space because I felt like I was suffocating in my own cocoon. I felt out of the loop of my own life while functioning like a silent thread in the fabric of the lives of others. I sought advice from everyone but trusted no one. One moment I thought I was seeing a light at the end of the tunnel, and the next I was being blinded by the headlights of an oncoming train.

Throughout it all I remained deeply concerned about maintaining control over my family, even though I was listless, empty,

and feeling like I wasn't all there. It was as if I'd been sucked into an emotional vacuum, becoming simply numb, unable to generate any kind of feeling for anyone or anything.

Unfortunately, this vacuum was all too obvious to the people closest to me, and they sought to fill it with their own well-meaning agendas on my behalf. It was much too easy for the boys to try to use this situation to their benefit, to go around me and get whatever they wanted, whether it was good for them or not. They were children and didn't know better; all they knew was that they had needs and those needs needed to be addressed. To be fair, it wasn't a case of "guys gone wild," but my mental and emotional state did little to reforge any family chain of command and little doubt was in my mind that I had become the weakest link.

This consensus was shared by those close personal relationships outside my immediate family. Since they had no way of understanding the full extent of what I was dealing with, they naturally thought to impose their own solutions and address their own needs from me as well. Nevertheless, I judge none of this because even bad leadership may be preferable to no leadership at all, at least when the intentions are good, which they were . . . whatever they were.

I wasn't sure what was wrong with me, but I didn't like the way I felt all the time. Thanks to the nanny, I still managed to take care of the boy's physical needs, but my own had begun to suffer terribly. I wasn't eating, I'd quit working out, I was smoking way too much. I could barely get motivated to get my work done, I was late with my deadlines, and I forgot things all the time.

Close friends and colleagues suggested I needed to be on anti-depressants and wondered why I wasn't taking them. Good question, but the thought of it only seemed to depress me even more.

Honestly, I just did not consider them to be an option, and as I think about why that was, or for that matter why I hadn't turned to alcohol or even drugs during a time when some people do as a distraction, I realize that the lessons I'd learned from Susan's strength were indirectly responsible, a lovely parting gift she'd left behind for me years ago, but one that only now I was finally beginning to get.

Shortly after her cancer was diagnosed and I was heavily involved in drawing *Ziggy* full-time, Susan began chemotherapy treatments. When they hadn't yet completely debilitated her, I had to fly to L.A. on an unavoidable business trip. I was reluctant to leave, and I remember still being dazed and overwhelmed by what had taken place in our lives because of the diagnosis. Susan's cancer had blindsided us, and still distracted, I was blindsided once again—by a Toyota Tercel that hit me as I was walking across La Brea Avenue.

To this day, I have no recollection of the actual accident or the bone-pulverizing impact that followed. One moment I was crossing La Brea Avenue in Los Angeles . . . and the very next, I was sitting in the middle of the street with my back propped up against a late model Toyota, trying to figure out why I couldn't stand up . . . was it natural for my foot to be twisted at a ninety-degree angle?

Obviously, I was in shock, though I didn't know it, and I felt absolutely no pain. I kept trying to get back on my feet. When I noticed my left leg had been twisted completely around, I remember just staring at it, still feeling no sensation or pain, and trying to make sense of what I was seeing. All the while I kept telling everyone around me, "It's okay, I'll be fine."

It wasn't until the paramedics were loading me onto the stretcher and into the ambulance that all of the missing pain flooded me with a vengeance, to the point that even the slightest jostle of the ambulance made me scream at the top of my lungs.

The doctors at Cedars-Sinai Hospital told me that my leg had been crushed and that a titanium rod had to be inserted and screwed in to hold my leg together. They said I'd eventually be able to walk again, possibly with a limp and needing a cane. I left Los Angeles and came home in a large plastic prosthesis that made me look like a half-assed version of the Bionic Man.

Upon my return, Susan was beginning to feel the effects of che-motherapy, but I was in a completely helpless state, constantly anesthetized with painkillers. While they did seem to help control the pain, they only added to the fact that I was a useless burden to my family at a time when they needed me most.

It took me almost a year to recover completely, to the point where I now am able to walk unassisted, and with only a small scar on my knee. But during that year of recovery, a large part of which I actually don't remember because of the drugs I was tak-ing, I was especially impacted by the positive example Susan set by walking each day, rain or shine, to keep her strength and energy going as she continued to fight the effects of cancer as well as the devastating aftereffects of her radical chemotherapy.

Seeing her leave the house, day in and day out, while I lay helpless and immobile on my useless butt, inspired me to even-tually join her on her daily walks. The initial pain I felt in taking each halting step forward was put into perspective by the pain I knew Susan was also experiencing and by the strength she exhib-ited in the constant positive steps forward she took to move beyond her illness.

I remember those walks as some of the most special and inspir-ing times we ever shared. It seemed we were able to draw support from each other when needed, and as I look back now, fully recovered and stronger than ever, I see how this was reminiscent of our life together as a whole.

Susan's courageous example of resilience and strength in the face of physical weakness and illness no doubt had a lot to do with my not getting on some form of medication when that dark depression hit. Let me be very clear about this: I know that antidepressants are very useful in treating people with clinical depression, but my personal choice, right or wrong, was not to go that route because of my previous experience with medications. They had left me incapacitated, which made me afraid of being even less effectual than I already was. I know in some cases it can be an absolute therapeutic necessity, but in my own circumstances, I didn't feel antidepressants were an option. Granted, I'm not a doctor, nor do I play one on TV, but I know it is supremely important to seriously consider the advice of your doctor when dealing with any form of depression.

As for me, I wasn't under a doctor's care, even if I should have been because I hated the way I felt. The oddest thing I remember was the overwhelming sense that my life was somehow unfinished and completely two-dimensional.

I felt like Ziggy, not his creator, trapped on a stained placemat at the Big Boy's table, abandoned by my Creator, and with no superheroes left to save me.

I prayed to heaven to please help me get my shit together. I was vulnerable and weak and felt like I was heading for a major fall. I wrote in my journal:

All aspects of my life appear to be converging upon some point in the very near future. What will happen to me? More important, what will happen to my children if I can't go on? I must, but how? The illness/depression will reach out and trap me. Why am I being subjected to these trials and tribulations? I've asked God and Susan to rescue me from this as if it's become a bad dream. If only I could wake up and everything, everyone would be as we were before the sickness entered our lives. I'm taking this journey against my will. Something so strong inside me is pulling me along; what is this force, where does it come from, where am I going so blindly? I pray now every night for some deliverance from this plague of inexistence. In the car I scream for help from Susan and God.

That's what I would do, it got so bad. I'd get into the car, roll up the windows, and drive so no one could hear me scream. It was as if I had been sucked into Alice's rabbit hole, a descent into a mad depression. The only question that remained was "How far down the rabbit hole was I willing to go?" I knew I needed to find my way out of this seemingly bottomless pit, the consuming darkness that had closed in so completely around me. I was desperate to take control of my life again, to find my lost focus, but how?

By chance, or perhaps *miraculously*, during this time that things were truly falling to pieces, an old friend of ours introduced me to a man she had been dating; he had also lost his wife to cancer. His process seemed very close to mine, and everything I was experiencing was something he had experienced—and had come through. He invited me to a grief counseling group.

I had gone to another such group, which the hospice had recommended, only a couple of weeks after Susan died. But frankly it was so depressing—people crying, and parents who had lost children to suicide or some other tragedy—that I couldn't bring myself to go back. Also, at that time, I had just gone into my Superman mode and couldn't imagine myself being the kind of emotional mess so many of these other people seemed to be.

By the time I went to this second grief group, I was a total mess. The counseling session gave me a tremendous sense of relief, because I discovered that the current professional opinion was that I was going through a major stress-inducing grief process. According to many in this group, all my responses and reactions, conscious or otherwise, were 100 percent textbook.

I was also gratified to be told that most of the problems I was experiencing were temporary and would gradually diminish over time. We touched upon a number of things in our session, including my childhood, my being a "fixer," caretaker, mediator, and martyr.

Perhaps, most significant, I was given some insights as to why I'd felt like a lunatic for the past few months. I was told that what I was feeling was absolutely normal for someone who has lost a spouse (what a relief!). In the months leading up to the anniversary of a beloved spouse's death, surviving spouses often go through a form of "temporary insanity," similar to Seasonal Affective Disorder (SAD). According to what I was told, after we experience a loss, often for years after at the same time of year, our subconscious relives in real time those tragic events that led up to the point of loss. Although our conscious self remains completely clueless, we fully experience the original emotional and physical repercussions, and we remain consciously unaware of the cause.

In my case, this "ghostly grief" begins its cycle approximately two months prior to the anniversary of Susan's death and increases in intensity over those two months.

When I attended this session, it was just a few weeks before Susan's death day, and clearly I had begun to reach critical mass. I looked so skeletal my friends worried that I was suffering from malnutrition. I knew that to survive this cycle and remain strong for those within the circle of my life, I would have to heal physically and mentally. Having already entered the rabbit hole and past the point of no return, I really had no choice but to continue to find my own way though this process.

In addition to gaining the realization that grief *is* a process, I realized that I had to gain as much understanding as possible about it so that I could learn to deal with the process more effectively. I was aware that many others had not only surrendered to their grief, but had even been destroyed by it. I have to believe

that at least part of the reason is because it's so difficult to see the big picture of what this grieving process truly is.

I came away from that counseling session with the knowledge that I had to resign myself, but never my life, to my grief.

Tragic loss is a lot like taking a grave detour along our path, but it's still not the path itself. What can present a challenge does not have to result in a defeat. As painful as this thing was, it became something of a backhanded gift, that, in time, offered opportunities for incredible personal rewards—once I learned to make it work, through patience and understanding, *for me* rather than *against me*.

Fully grasping what had become something of an epiphany for me, I became determined that I could *not* be defeated and that I had the opportunity to emerge as a better person, more whole than I ever would have been without these unexpected challenges, which offered me no easy first answers to cushion my spinning-out-of-control skid off the highway of life.

Another epiphany was the realization that the only way I could eventually walk away from this depression was to turn my rudder into it and ride out the process of this storm. Similar to the effects of shock I had experienced during my accident, I needed to use this time positively to gain a greater awareness of what was taking place in my life and try to see depression as something of an anesthetic, or even a form of suspended animation, that would allow me to weather the onslaught of grief and pain as they continued to hit me with their best shots. If I could do that, I could reinforce, rebuild, and move forward in my quest to overcome this great challenge. By gaining such a perspective, I was able to see my mind, body, and spirit as allies rather than adversaries. After all, aren't we in the same boat?

Journal Entry

November 1

Progress Report:

I've begun to realize that taking time to continue mourning is necessary. I've been doing this quite a bit lately. I'll listen to music and think of Susan; I've begun to realize it's really okay to cry at the thought of her and the mention of her name. I need to say good-bye to the past, not by ignoring it or pretending it never existed, but to honor and treasure it and all that Susan has meant to me. When I do this I feel a deeper appreciation for my wonderful children and what a great vestige of our union they truly are.

When I think of Susan I feel her around me, guiding things within this process. I know with little effort I could get lost in mourning over her and it could become an all-consuming grief. I still can't believe that I'll not ever see her again in my lifetime. Receiving the most from our present and our future means forgiving, but not forgetting our past.

When one sees their life as an amalgam of experiences past, present, and future, it is easier to sense a larger plan for oneself in every moment. I see Synchronicity as well as Cause and Effect. This is very comforting.

There are clues and signs available that show us that part of our plan includes getting beyond our pain and finding an intended future. Working within this framework means neither denying the past nor racing through the present.

Today's present will always become tomorrow's past, and this present moment is the place where our future and our past coalesce. If I have within me the power to influence my present with a simple positive thought, then I can simultaneously create a more positive past and future, as well.

"Go with the flow" may be a trite and dated saying, but it is a valid idea. Fighting the current and panicking in the water is exhausting and leads to drowning. By letting the current of the process simply carry me, eventually it may lead to a better place of personal growth and emotional well-being.

What if I choose to cease struggling and just allow the current to carry me for a while, using this time to build back my strength in order to create a better future and live to fight another day?

What if I just enjoy what my past with Susan has given me, the way a lover reminisces and savors a magic evening of love?

What if I just enjoy the wonder of being a father to two incredible young children? What if I just enjoy the company of my friends and family?

What if I just enjoy the fantastic job I have and make the very most of it?

WHAT IF I just enjoy this wonderful life I've been blessed with and not only "GO with the FLOW," but learn to "GLOW with the FLOW"?

Life is a love affair and love is an affair of life. Love affairs must be embraced and savored for all their complexities, just as life must be, as well. Being a student of life also means being a student of love. Love is a living thing with an agenda and a commission to work within our fate. Susan and I are forever linked and she will continue to guide me through the lessons we learned together. In this way, Susan and our love will always be alive in me on this plain as she continues to live on in another.

I miss holding you, Susan, but I feel you holding me still.

Armed with the consoling new understanding that this time of year was just naturally going to be difficult for some time to come, and with my physical and mental reserves all but depleted, I decided the Three Amigos were going to spend a couple of weeks taking a vacation in Hawaii, a place none of us had ever been before, nor ever anticipated we one day might. Whether by coincidence or design, like a smoldering volcano, the first anniversary of Susan's death fell dead center on our time in this island paradise.

I remember thinking that I was going to resolve myself to the fact that however difficult it may be, this day was going to become the first milestone dedicated to marking a positive turning point in my entire grieving process, one that would set a precedent for each year to come.

The morning of the anniversary found me up to meet the sunrise. I walked the virgin beach and waded into the peaceful warm waters of the Pacific Ocean to say my farewells to my depression, my lost love, and my lost life. Casting a handful of native flowers into the surf, I watched it carry them away as I whispered loving words to Susan, along with a prayer of new understanding to God.

What I hadn't expected was that this would become so much more than just another day in paradise. I felt all of the accumulated stress and unconscious turmoil miraculously wash away from me, leaving only conscious and positive memories to carry me through the coming year, and what remained of my new and uncertain life.

As I turned back toward the empty beach behind me, I noticed the meandering trail of my single set of footprints in the sand . . . and in that moment of awareness, I not only felt God with me again, but understood that He had never left my side.

When we returned from Hawaii, I spent the first day back home unpacking our suitcases, doing piles of laundry, and looking for a place to keep some memorabilia, like ticket stubs and island maps that held too many good memories to lose. I put everything into a folder and decided to file it away in a little-used bureau drawer where Susan and I had always kept our own paper trail of travels together.

I opened the drawer and found a greeting card envelope. On the front, in Susan's uneven script, were the words: TO TOMMY. When Susan had placed this there, I have no idea. But the very shaky handwriting meant it could only have been written to me very shortly before she died.

My own hands, now shaking, carefully opened the sealed envelope. I was acutely aware that the lips that had last touched it were those I had kissed ten thousand times over twenty-two beautiful years, and were now sealed forever—except for these last words that awaited me. I slid the greeting card from the envelope.

In stunned disbelief, my jaw dropped when I saw the card's cover embossed with the image of a beach . . . along with the *Footprints* poem. Inside, obviously at great pain to herself, Susan had managed to leave me her last words:

Tommy, I love you so much, but that pales in the light of the Almighty. He and His love are with you wherever you go. You are not alone!

Love, Susan

OUTWARD . . .

I'VE JUST CHANGED LANES here again on I-71, probably put about twenty more miles behind me, and it occurs to me for, oh, maybe the tenth time in as many minutes, that a tall cup of coffee would sure be nice to keep me company. Not just any coffee, mind you, because, man, do I like that Starbucks.

Despite being behind schedule, I'm craning my head at every exit, impatiently searching the horizon for that familiar green and white sign. Finally, I reach an exit, just like a hundred others, and I'm pulling off on a road I haven't taken before . . . passing all the familiar Clown, King, and Colonel joints . . . and now I'm thinking, *Well, I'll drive a little farther.*

Another mile goes by, same thing, still looking. It's starting to put a major dent in the time I mentally allocated to get off the highway and get back on my journey. But I've got this much time and distance into it now, so I might as well keep driving . . . into what looks like a very beautiful little town.

I enter the town center: stately Victorian buildings; a town square, classic old bandstand in the center, painted white; quaint little shops. And I'm still looking for the damn Starbucks. The crazy thing is, I'm circling this town square, and I've already passed three really cute small coffee shops. These are not franchises, they're not large businesses: they're ma-and-pa stores. Somebody's dream, someone's idea of what they've always wanted to do. And even in a world of gourmet coffee chains, it's nice to know there are still places like Susan's Coffee Shop (no lie, that's the real name). I pass Susan's twice, still desperately seeking Starbucks, until I finally realize that I'm simply not going to get my way.

So I park the car, get out, and head for Susan's.

Right next door is an old bookstore. And boom! There, in the front window, is a book I've been looking for everywhere but could never find on the chain bookstores' shelves. I make a note to go in and get it, but first things first.

Susan's coffee shop is a beautiful little place that makes you feel welcome and right at home the moment you enter. Inhaling the wonderfully rich aromas, I tell the pretty barista that Susan's House Blend will do.

She delivers my steaming hot brew "to go," with a flourish and a smile. A father, holding the hand of his little boy, who's wearing a Superman T-shirt under his open jacket, enters the store as I'm about to leave. I feel a pang of nostalgia as we chat for a few minutes before I head next door, get my book, and step back into the night.

My thoughts turn to my own two sons as I return to my car and shoot back to the highway. Speeding my way home, I'm thinking about detours and how worthwhile this one was. To tell you the truth, this is the best-tasting coffee I can ever remember, perhaps because it's blended with the discovery of a beautiful little town I hadn't intended to visit and warm, friendly people I otherwise wouldn't have met, even if only in passing.

Like caffeine, I tend to get addicted to my routines, becoming resistant to change. Maybe we all do to some extent. It's so easy to plan our journey and fix our eyes straight ahead, focused on our destination, while we miss what's around us, including the signs we're really looking for but are in too much of a hurry to notice.

I love this coffee. And I'm loving the idea, the feeling here that things hoped for, though not easily seen, can become much more valuable to us than what we are accustomed to and take for granted, no matter how great the familiar feels. Taking that detour, whether intended or not, on our journey can make all the difference in life.

In my mind's eye, Ziggy agrees with a nod before offering his simple, Zen-like take on the subject: "Every now and then, maybe we become lost in order to find ourselves again."

From personal experience, I know there's a lot of truth to that. And as I savor another hot sip, I find myself wondering if sometimes it's the unfamiliar grounds that make us feel most at home.

* * *

I have a vague recollection of an old Hawaiian saying that if you cast an unconditional gift into the ocean, it returns to you sevenfold. I'm no Big Kahuna, but I will say that from the very day marking that first anniversary, I detected a sea change in the direction my life seemed to be flowing.

After feeling all that weight of worry and guilt and grief washed from me, I was more than grateful; I felt renewed. While not completely understanding this process and how things worked at the time, in very simple Ziggy terms, he says it best: "Worry is like a rocking chair, it gives you something to do but it really doesn't get you anywhere."

As I watched the surf lapping up and down the endless expanse of the empty shore, carrying the wild island flowers I'd thrown in farther out with each ebb and flow, I was again reminded of the zigzagging pattern not only of life and death, but also of understanding and growth—an ever-moving path and process that strikes me as serpentine in nature, as well. One of Susan's favorite sayings from the Bible was "Be wise as serpents and harmless as doves" (Matthew 10:16).

Her verse takes on new meaning in light of the personal, and professional, path I've been on for such a long time. Not unlike an old Ziggy maxim that says, "I guess I Zigged when I should've Zagged." The fact of the matter is, even if our lives take a turn for the worse or go down what seems to be the wrong path, every Zig will ultimately lead to a Zag, and every Zag to another Zig.

On the same trip marking that first anniversary, just about everything in my own life seemed to take a positive turn. A significant turn for the better actually began with one of the most intense and realistic nightmares I have ever had. I was sleeping in the hotel bed one minute, then wide-awake the next, startled upright and lathered in sweat. Still throbbing in my mind was this horrible vision that after having had my future with Susan stolen away, all of my other hopes and dreams had been taken from me as well. I remember feeling as if not only had I just lost my life, but somebody else had found it and managed to make it work better than I had.

This nightmare was particularly specific about an idea I'd had for some time concerning the creation of a new business, specializing in the development of characters for other businesses and brands. Although this was a dear and long-held dream of mine, I had put it on the back burner for the past eight years because of everything we had been dealing with. In my nightmare, some sneaky bastard had done the exact same company, developed it in every detail exactly as I had conceived it, even to the point of calling it by the same name.

Groggy and confused, I did a quick reality check. I can't describe my relief to realize that it was all just a bad dream. So what was holding me back now? I began scribbling down every thought, memory, and idea I had originally conceived regarding what soon became Character Matters. When I returned to the mainland, I began the groundwork necessary to bring my new business to life.

I'm still amazed at how it took a nightmare to wake me up to the rest of my life. Dreams, I've come to learn, can be very powerful creations, and the only one who can keep me from my dreams is myself.

In my professional life I became excited with a new kind of zeal I'd never known before. I stepped-up my speaking engagements and got more involved in nonprofit organizations, such as Boys and Girls Town, USA.

I began to no longer see my world as a two-dimensional box, and I traveled to places I'd never been: Paris, Las Vegas, and Marceline, Missouri, to name a few. And wherever I went, I saw with new eyes, a new perspective, these places and the people I met there.

I remember Paris, a day I spent at the Louvre. It was there that

I saw the great works of Leonardo da Vinci, but I viewed them as a student of life rather than as a life student of art. As a master of the twin techniques of light and shade, Leonardo intimately understood the defining power of shadow, that great intangible that can only exist within a perfect balance between darkness and light, the known and the unknown. From my background in art history, I knew Leonardo called this "engaging the shadow," but now I found myself wondering, *Why do we live in a full-spectrum world yet often only see it in shades of black and white?* And I realized that just as Leonardo believed true illumination emanates from within, we too have the ability to draw from ourselves a delicate balance of self-awareness, one that comes from both our dark *and* our light sides by engaging the shadow within us.

In Las Vegas I woke up very early one morning and went down to the casino for coffee—and, of all things, to write. In what was my third, or possibly fourth, journal, I noted:

Ah, yes, Las Vegas: Where people clean out the rooms after the rooms are finished cleaning out the people. Within the massive complex of Caesars Palace, so alive with chaos the night before, I'm seeing a quiet and simple order this early morning. Someone meticulously polishes marble columns. Humming vacuum cleaners and floor polishers cover every square inch of floor. I'm watching a very small ancient woman dusting and wiping away fingerprints on endless rows of slot machines.

Aside from a few burned-out, chain-smoking gamblers still at the tables, a beautiful organized dance takes place in the small hours of the new dawn. It speaks to this new awakening I feel inside of myself that makes me want to seize the day and grow in every way possible. I feel an urgency to make up for lost time. I feel as if I've not only been brought back from the dead, but as if a great part of me was dead and buried for most of my life and has now been resurrected and released by confronting the unfamiliar and the unknown.

I am a creative spirit, I live for the stuff, and it has great potential for helping others and myself. I believe in who I am, what I've become. I see the world at work in my life; I see my life at work in the world. Millions of people draw strength from what I do every day drawing Ziggy, and as I begin to feel my way around the walls of my world, building and reinforcing them, I mustn't forget that those walls also have doors and windows into the worlds of so many lives; all must be thrown open wide. I will try to build something wonderful and try to keep my balance as I build. God gives us all what we need to reach our potential, but the skill and understanding of how to use these tools is what we all have to learn.

While on the surface this particular entry might not seem all that important, something had changed in my journaling. Instead of constantly looking inward and writing about things that were happening *to* me, I began to immerse myself in the moment and look outward, to think in terms of how I could be the one to *make* things happen instead.

As for Marceline, Missouri, I had the honor of being named Grand Marshal for their yearly Toonfest. You see, Marceline is the boyhood home of Walt Disney. And it was there that I sat beneath what Walt had called his "Dreaming Tree," a place where a young boy envisioned great dreams he would eventually bring to life. Despite many hardships he endured, in 1955 Disney saw his vision of Disneyland become a reality. Sitting beneath Walt's Dreaming Tree is like getting sprinkled with Tinker Bell's pixie dust, and I can only liken that moment, and the days I shared with the warm, gracious people in Marceline, to pure magic.

The point is that even simple things I might have taken for granted before became experiences to savor. I became fully immersed with life on a whole different level. I took renewed delight in raising my sons (who turned some corners of their own), my new business, meeting new people, and appreciating each new day as a source of discovery and wonder.

I wish I could say that after turning such a pivotal corner on that first anniversary I was able to move forward without any debilitating bouts of depression over Susan's death, but that would be a lie. As I'd been cautioned in the grief counseling group, anyone who has lost someone near to them can experience a recurrence of these feelings even years later.

I certainly did . . . and often still do.

For me, initially at least, all it took was something as simple as walking alone through the grocery store my wife and I used to walk through together. I would pick up some Cap'n Crunch cereal for the kids—well, I always told Susan it was for the kids—then I would start crying in the aisles and not know why. Why is a freaking box of Cap'n Crunch cereal bringing me to tears? And frankly, you know it's not the yellow dye #3. Or the fact that the Captain is so damn cute.

Often we naturally classify certain things as negative simply because they are intimately associated with something painful. Grief, mourning, or whatever we want to call it is associated with terrible experiences, so it seems natural to assume this reaction is terrible, too—something to be pushed away and avoided as much as the experience that caused it. What I've learned, at least with this particular kind of depression, is quite the opposite.

In certain cases, I think depression can actually be a positive experience rather than a negative one. Seriously, I believe depression sometimes gets a bum rap. Not clinical depression, of course; as I've said, I would never minimize the trauma such an illness can cause for its sufferers and their families. What I'm referring to is situational depression that comes from a severe loss or other traumatic event that rocks the foundation of our world.

I'm reminded again of my accident on La Brea Avenue in L.A. It wasn't until after the shock from the impact had worn off and the aftershock of excruciating pain hit that I began to realize just how grateful I was for going into shock. Every moment of numbed freedom from that agony, no matter how brief, was a gift to me, a blessing rather than a curse.

This understanding, a souvenir from a previous detour along my life path, ultimately helped me to perceive my grief and depression over Susan's death in a similar way: a blessing from a loving Creator, whom I had all but blasphemed and denied, rather than a continuing torment and punishment from a monstrous and uncaring deity.

In my case, grieving became the emotionally suppressed equivalent of physical trauma shock—a depression-based Pit Stop or Time Out of Mind, where, with my passions and emotions temporarily nullified, I could step outside of myself and my pain, assess my overall situation, and locate a positive and possibly lifesaving course of action to pursue.

At first it's damn frustrating to feel like your life has come to a complete halt and the rest of the world is passing you by. Getting back on track and back up to speed after it seems that life has done a "drive-by" on us can be difficult, too. Taking that Pit Stop gives us a little time-out to let everything under the hood cool down before we blow a gasket, completely break down, or worse . . . become unsafe at any speed.

Experience has taught me that if we can confront depression rather than try to deny or avoid its existence, then this Pit Stop can actually become an opportunity to decide how best to handle the rest of our lives. It's a matter of perspective, thinking about this difficult time as a very special, bittersweet gift—especially when it's easy to become obsessed with obsession and sometimes even grief, which in itself becomes a way to ignore the root cause of internalized pain.

Journaling forced me, albeit unknowingly at the time, to look inward to find understanding, strength, and that hero I was in search of, without avoiding the subsequent depression I dearly wanted to outmaneuver. Journaling made a huge difference for me, and has led me to believe that, ironically, depression can sometimes be part of the cure *not* just part of the pain.

People who knew me in "the bad old days" and see me now still wonder how going through something so awful could possibly be beneficial in any way. It's a fair question. But fair is a relative term dependent on one's perspective at the time, and life isn't always fair.

Although my own perspective has changed dramatically on so many things, I still at times struggle to see that some good and self-growth can come out of a terrible personal loss. The trick, I've learned, is to view these periods of depression that can crop up out of nowhere as a vehicle for long-term healing instead of an opportunity to seek out and encourage new distractions to make the world go away. The fact is the world will never go away, at least not until we do, and as long as we continue to try to avoid it, neither will the emptiness, aloneness, and numbness that are characteristics of depression. The only choice we truly have is *how* we choose to deal with our pain.

Whether or not we get to be behind the wheel of our own Karma, we can utilize the gift of a crossroads where we stop, look, listen, and eventually move on with whatever lessons we might be able to sift from the rubble of lost love or shattered dreams.

One would think that once we start moving forward, we should continue moving ahead with escalating speed. Not necessarily. It's not always "downhill from here" when coming out of depression. Sometimes it's important to pull over, put on the parking brake, and take stock to carry on with awareness and understanding instead of denial and amnesia. To know where we are going, we need to know where we are and where we've been.

We can't hide from ourselves; we can't outrun our pain. It will

never stop pursuing us. No matter how fast or how far we travel to put that pain behind us, it's always there, a backseat driver waiting for us to look in our rearview mirrors, where images are closer than they appear.

It's a lot like the overdue movie rental that's been sitting under a mountain of bills on your desk for the past month, quietly racking up those late fees. At first, you avoid taking it back because you just don't want to make the trip. Before you know it, those late fees, overdue reminder notes, and automated phone calls harass you to the point where you say, "Jeez, I don't even want to go in there and have to pay." Eventually, you know that if you don't settle up soon, you'll never show your face in that video rental place again. Hell, you might even move!

In the blockbuster match with this heavyweight called depression, we make the call in the end. We decide whether we're down for the count, whether we'll let it keep us pinned against the ropes before knocking us out, or if we're going to use those ropes to pull ourselves up and fight our way to a comeback.

Creating anything inspiring must first begin with a positive vision. In painful times, the clock keeps ticking, moving forward to an anticipated future when our greatest troubles have become only a memory and we view them as an experience of living this life.

Besides my battle with depression, I had something else to come to terms with, and that was my perception of *miracles*. Throughout our lives, when things get tough, we find ourselves calling upon the gods or heroes we know to bring us miracles. But when our path doesn't seem to work out the way we planned it, when those miracles don't arrive as quickly or in the manner in which we expected, we can easily lose faith in what we believe. But you know what? Seeing is not believing. Believing is seeing.

I believed, for a while, that God took my faith when he took my beloved wife from me, but what I came to realize is that I had never lost my ability to have faith. It became enough for me to believe that, even in the moments I didn't know God, couldn't fathom His purpose, couldn't forgive what I perceived as His lack of miraculous action, somehow God knew *me*.

Every moment is miraculous, and the value of any moment depends upon how it is lived. Every moment exists as potential— from miracle to misery. God creates the moment, and within it we discover the potential miracle. A miraculous process . . . not a processed miracle.

Albert Einstein once said that he didn't believe God plays dice with the universe; in other words, life is not a game of chance. And while it's also been said that life is a crapshoot (and plenty of crap can come down that shoot), what I think also needs to be said is that every moment we're here is one more roll of the dice, another miraculous act of creation.

Every one of us alive today is like a lucky gambler. Each of us is the generational end product of thousands upon thousands of lucky rolls of life's dice. You and I are living proof of divinely inspired good fortune by being the end result of our ancestors surviving every plague, famine, war, cataclysm, and disaster throughout human history.

Odds are that we live our lives on purpose. It is not due to random chance or dumb luck—it's nothing short of a miracle that, in this very moment, we are all here together, collective jackpot winners of the right to assume ownership of our lives and to take possession of the purpose and meaning behind them.

Recently, I came across a folded piece of paper a friend handed to me at the end of Susan's funeral. It was her eulogy notes. In part, they read:

"I know nothing." That was Susan's favorite quote from our Course in Miracles study group. It made her laugh to think that Colonel Klink's line from Hogan's Heroes *would pop up in a spiritual context. And yet, by knowing nothing, Susan could suspend judgment and accept things as they are. She could send love even to people who behaved rudely, seeing them merely as troubled souls. She could stay firmly rooted in the moment.*

I know nothing.

Our challenge is to love as Susan loved. To hold those we love tightly to our hearts and bones as though our lives and their lives depend on it, and to be able to let them go, realizing that we will always know nothing.

Every now and then we have the good fortune of meeting someone or discovering something that can radically change our lives for the better. If we think of these people or these places or these things as miracles unto themselves, we realize that they're part of a process as well—a process in which all of us are connected. It's the simple understanding that each one of us represents those small connecting points that become the miraculous path of living.

Everything is constantly moving, constantly changing, and perhaps the best way to navigate our way through it all is to understand that the only thing that *never* changes is change itself. My own process in the miracle of healing began with my understanding that while everything changes, my perception needed to change occasionally, too, especially when things no longer went according to plan or when I realized that my plans were no longer leading me where I wished to go. My healing process took a big leap forward when I made a conscious decision to allow myself to become a part of that change rather than to resist it.

Why it took me so long to come to this realization is a mystery because the best example of resilience in the face of change and uncertainty has been with me most of my life.

Ziggy has made a living out of basically getting through every bad thing imaginable over his lifetime, and as a result, Ziggy has changed his loser status to a character who inspires people, a guide of sorts. But ironically, or maybe not so ironically, he became my guide, too.

Ziggy is not just a two-dimensional character, not just a job, but a friend who I had once erroneously thought was dependant upon me, when in reality, when I most needed somebody, he was there for me to depend on. He showed me that by continuing to deal with life, we can find a better way to overcome our problems simply by hanging in there, and *that* brings new strength, new understanding, and in the end, helps us create a better version of ourselves.

Ziggy, to me, is art come to life in many ways. He became an ever-present source of strength and comfort in my darkest days when I was expecting some help or miracle from a whole other place.

I have to admit that while Ziggy was always there for me, I was not always there for him. It is hard to draw from life once you've begun to withdraw from it, and in those "darkest days," my world had become so flat, lifeless, and uninspired that I withdrew not only from my world, but also from the responsibility of having to create Ziggy's.

My syndicate editors were beginning to express their concern that my publication lead time—the amount of cartoons completed and submitted ahead of their actual due date—was dwindling weekly. Over so many consecutive years of completing and sending my Ziggy cartoons ahead of schedule or on time for editing, printing, distribution, and publication, I had successfully created a surplus of submitted comic strips, which granted me a

comfortable safety margin against missing every syndicated cartoonist's worst nightmare: the ever present "Deadline!"

In the case of black-and-white "daily" (Monday–Saturday)
comic strips, the absolute minimum deadline is two weeks prior
to their appearance in newspapers. And for Sunday comic features, due to the additional steps required for color printing, the
firm deadline is seven weeks ahead of newspaper publication. To
miss this submission deadline by even one day will result in significant late fees to the cartoonist. In addition to the fines, if a
feature is consistently late, the individual newspaper comic page
editors will deem the feature "unreliable" and drop it from their
newspaper's comic section.

During my "Superman" phase immediately following Susan's
death, and for many months thereafter, I had been producing
comic strips, sending them in early, and fortifying my lead time.
I even remember actually being proud that I took only one week
off from drawing to make Susan's burial arrangements and attend
her funeral.

Now, however, things were different. I had no energy, no passion, no emotion, and found it almost impossible to motivate
myself to work. As the weeks wore on and my deadline crept closer,
the letters, e-mails, and phone calls from my syndicate became more
insistent. For my part, that problem took care of itself as I employed

a brilliant solution to deal with it: I simply didn't deal with it. I didn't open the letters, open my e-mail, or answer the phone.

I was becoming a real recluse. Friends had all but given up trying to call me, which was fine with me because it meant no more of those annoying ringing sounds coming from my phone. I had also officially broken up with Lois for the third or fourth last time, so I was no longer going out on dates, and I had all but given up going to the gym to work out.

With each passing day, the twin stacks of unopened mail and unfinished *Ziggy* work on my desk mounted—until one day the stacks collapsed under the weight of one unaddressed warning too many. I just stood there, staring blank faced at the mess my inattention to responsibility had made. But I remained in my indifference and inaction. I remember wondering where my passion had gone, why it had gone, and what would possibly have to happen to stir any kind of emotion within me again.

The following morning, on September 11, 2001, I switched on the TV and watched in disbelief as the first . . . and then the second plane hit the twin towers. I watched helplessly, along with a helpless world, as those two great pillars of steel collapsed under their own weight and fell in upon each other. In a moment, both were swallowed by a huge, undulating cloud of smoke and spirit, pulsating upward to span the distance between heaven and what could only be described as hell on earth.

Over the weeks that followed, I watched, as did we all, doing little else, as this unbelievable nightmare continued to unfold. My loss of Susan and the path I had taken since her death struck a sharp contrast to the cataclysmic act of destruction, the heart-wrenching human reactions to overwhelming loss, the ongoing yet increasingly desperate search for survivors, answers, evidence of guilt . . . and finally, the desire and absolute need for healing, closure, and moving on from tragedy.

As I continued to watch on television the horrific reruns of the initial attack, collapse, and rescue operations, I began to recognize my overwhelming feeling of helplessness, which was much like I had felt as Susan lay dying. I also recognized my feelings of blind hatred and anger at God now being directed toward the as yet unseen, unknown, and apparently untouchable criminal mastermind responsible for this hideous and unjust act.

My childishness and behavior toward God were also brought into pinpoint focus. Had I really reserved the same hatred and anger for my Creator that I now directed toward Osama bin Laden? How dare I? Was I nuts?

Those inspiring images of everyday heroes tirelessly digging through the rubble that was once two towering twins continued to pass before my eyes, and for the first time in a long time, I sat at my desk in front of the television, rolled up my sleeves, and pulled out the most recent letters from the collapsed piles of correspondence before me. I knew what was buried beneath that mound was neglected responsibility and the guilt I bore over it. Just beginning to open those things felt oppressively overwhelming. Apparently denial worked in my favor for only so long, and now it was time to pay not only a ton of overdue bills, but the piper as well.

The news was not good. My lead time on *Ziggy* was depleted, and the deadline for new work had already come and gone. Not only was I late . . . I was very late, and newspaper editors were beginning to complain. Ziggy was now in real danger, and he desperately needed me to rescue him as much as I needed him to save me.

After I opened the last piece of mail, and paid the last bill, what remained was a large stack of incomplete *Ziggy* panels. Looking up from the top panel was the familiar image of my successful little brother. He looked so fragile, faint, and unfinished that I began to wonder how I could possibly take for granted something that was so precious to my father as well as to so many other people.

Was it because I never really felt Ziggy was a part of me since I hadn't been his original creator? Did I not truly appreciate Ziggy because once he became successful, that success demanded so much of my dad's time and attention that it took him away from me when I needed him in my formative years?

The more I thought about all of this, the more nauseous I felt about how I had placed my innocent little brother in jeopardy. I wondered, had he been able, would Ziggy have hated and blasphemed me, accused me of turning away from him as I had done toward my own Creator? Or would he, in his own naïve and childlike way, somehow understand and still love me?

Aware of how close to disaster my actions, or my inaction, had drawn him, my mind returned to those wonderful Big Boy days when SAVE ZIGGY! on a placemat had been my father's unconditional gift of love just for me. I knew that I had always loved this beautiful little character and Ziggy would know I could never abandon him. I understood that he had never divided me from my father, because Ziggy not only brought us closer to each other, he had united us all.

Picking up my pen, I began drawing Ziggy, and through him, myself back to life. I did this as I continued to watch the television, witnessing the heroic acts of firemen, policemen, paramedics, and everyday citizens unconditionally risking, and often losing everything, by running headfirst into hell to save lives. I realized that *real* superheroes actually do exist, and they don't need to wear capes.

In his own way, Ziggy did save me from myself, and he helped me see how misplaced my anger was toward God. Really, everything I ever needed to get through those dark days was with me already. I just had to go the distance on a very long and difficult journey to find that my destination—and Ziggy—had been along for the ride the whole time.

God never abandoned me. He was just patiently waiting for me to understand how truly prophetic those words of *Footprints* were. Making that discovery resulted in a paradigm shift in my understanding of many of the things about which I once became very disillusioned. Tragedy is always going to happen. Like those who lost so much during 9/11, it's up to us to figure out how best to deal with life's tragedies and go on. There are various ways and everyone has their own, but if we feel we've been abandoned, that we're alone and nobody cares, maybe it's only because we don't see things the way they really are. That perspective helped me find and look forward to a new future, a new life journey, when I had felt I would have none.

You know, the destination is always the heart of the journey through life, and the journey home is about beating a path to its door. To find our path, sometimes we need to lose our way, which I certainly did, to discover that we only know where we are going when we finally get there. My personal journey has not been an easy one, but I'm living proof that some remarkably wonderful things can still remain with us even after the one we love most dies.

We may lose friends, hopes, dreams, and loved ones along the way, but they're always a part of us. And the memories, strengths, and lessons they've given to us are gifts we can still learn from even when we are parted. But they're only gifts if we stop looking for what we expect to see and start to appreciate what is actually there, the miraculous process of life unfolding.

I am blessed by God through the wonderful gifts given, and lessons taught to me by all the people I've come to know. Though Susan has departed from this world and my father doesn't seem to always recognize me anymore, their presence will remain with me forever.

It's true when tragedy strikes or misfortune happens in our lives, when unexpected things take us on detours from the path we've set for ourselves, those things we don't see coming affect us the most. That is a fact of life. But one of the miracles of life is that if it's what we don't see coming that can hit us the hardest, it's what we don't always immediately see within ourselves that can help us the most. It turns out that not only do we have everything inside us to carry on from the beginning of a lifetime to the end of it, we also have the resources within us to begin life again after life ends.

Alone on that beach in Hawaii, with the sun of a new day rising before me, I no longer felt alone. I knew that even though there are times when life feels empty, it's anything but empty. Life is full of living. And when you get down to it, the journey we make is only as important as those wonderful spirits we meet along the way, whether they come from relationships, true loves, or simple angels unaware that pass through our lives.

All of them live on within us and each of them is a gift from God. And even when they leave us, the finest and most loving way we can honor them is to keep them with us as we continue on, remembering that every detour, no matter how difficult or out of the way it may take us, always leads back home, that place we keep deep inside us, where it's always been.

HOMEWARD . . .

STILL BARRELING THROUGH THE darkness on this last stretch of highway home, I just got off my cell phone. I was talking to an old friend I haven't spoken with in more than six months. It is a privilege knowing this fellow cartoonist, a great talent, and really super guy. Shortly before we last saw each other, he lost someone very dear to him. I told him that if he ever needed to talk to another person who had come from a similar place, who was maybe a little bit farther down the same road, he should give me call.

Well, tonight, out of the blue, he did. He told me he was feeling completely lost. He said that he felt two-dimensional, like he was living in a comic strip—God, déjà vu all over again—that he felt like he wasn't in control of his own life and was feeling extremely depressed. As I listened to him and told him my story, albeit the Cliffs Notes version, I could sense him gaining some peace from knowing he wasn't alone, that even bad things can have a purpose. I reassured him that, like anything along life's highway, this too will pass.

This man is my age. He's a successful cartoonist. He lost a woman he loved and now feels lost himself. In many ways he is a mirror image of me, and yet tonight I was given a rearview mirror, the perspective of hindsight to see where I've been, while my friend, who feels detoured down a dead end and going nowhere fast, was given a forward view of what lies ahead.

People really can be mirrors to one another. As I think about the things we discussed, like perspective, purpose, and path, it makes me appreciate the embarrassment of riches I have, especially those waiting at home.

So I just put in a quick call to the boys, letting them know I can't wait to see them but I'm going to be later than usual. We'll have cause to celebrate when I get there because Miles just aced some college exams and Sam had some other exciting news about his involvement in a project at school, where he's the senior class president.

I take great pride in their accomplishments, as all loving parents do in their kids. But I'm intimately acquainted with their own personal adversities in life, which probably makes me prouder than most. I can't help but brag about them; they've turned out to be such fine young men. As for how I'll handle it once they've left the nest, your guess is as good as mine, but I'd rather not think about that now.

After all, I'm in a grace period, and I can appreciate small luxuries like knowing I'm not the only thing turning up overdue tonight. Miles and Sam told me that they finally found the lost *Spiderman* rental buried under the mess on my desk. I told them to go ahead and watch it without me, but Miles said they'd rather wait until I get there so we can all see it together.

I'm not that crazy about seeing Spiderman when I get home, but I am about seeing those two super boys, well on their way to becoming grown men.

Funny how the more some things change, the more they remain the same. I had Superman; they have Spiderman!

We've had so many superheroes, each one arriving at their superpowers through some horrible accident, chain of events, or trauma—usually involving a nuclear reactor or something radioactive, which gets tiring after a while. But Superman had a planet blow up under him, and that's about as bad as it gets in the way of disasters. On his home planet he was a regular guy, nothing special, but when he comes to Earth all that changes, and he finds himself with these incredible powers and abilities far beyond those of us mere mortals.

He can fly, leap tall buildings in a single bound, and that x-ray vision thing always intrigued me when I was a kid, especially because it was natural to wonder if Superboy ever used his super vision to do a little "supervision" on the girls in the Smallville High locker room. Probably not. That would be a little too human and purely human Superman is not.

If any of us were indestructible, if no bullet could pierce us, no enemy defeat us, if with our super vision we could see everything there is to see . . . where would our own humanity be? Where would our point of empathy be? Granted, Superman had empathy for the human condition, and I believe that's why he was always super in our eyes. But without the Kryptonite, without the longing and unrequited love of Lois Lane, without the internal conflict of Clark Kent, Superman would be completely indestructible, and no humanness would be in him and, therefore, no point of empathy for us. In terms of our caring for Superman, it's less about the "super" than it is about the "man" that gives him his vulnerabilities and allows us to identify with him. Despite Superman's many gifts, we don't love him for his struggles with archvillains, but because he also struggles with the same things each of us struggles with every day.

Superman's cape was his spectacle, while Clark's spectacles were his cape. Superman wanted to be human; he valued and strove to embrace what we feel are our weaknesses—while we strive to be super, embracing what we feel are our strengths.

For Superman, the transition from Average Joe Six-Pack on his planet to a six-packed superhero on ours was a direct result of his world literally coming apart. Our own transition to superhero usually happens when our worlds come apart, as well. Losing what we love most, just as Superman lost all he knew and loved, can force us to look within and find hidden powers we had no idea we possessed. Yet when we do return to Earth and our feet are back on the ground, we are issued a great challenge: to find the balance between the Man of Steel within and the mortal without.

Maybe that's why this character will always be with us, representing our dreams of an ideal self, why children will be wearing those Superman T-shirts over their little bodies for years and years to come. Dreaming. Believing.

For women, the search may be for ruby slippers. For men, it may be a pair of Viagra-blue underwear with a big red S. But we are all on the same journey to find that place inside where we feel we are truly at home with ourselves, the place we treasure most in a world full of chaos. We're those little boys in their Superman T-shirts, dreaming of being supermen one day like their fathers, and their fathers dreaming of being supermen for their little girls, little boys, all the people they care about, in a world where they're forced to live as Clark Kent.

But you know what? The *real* superheroes are the single parents doing their best to raise their kids alone. They're the faithful husbands, the loving mothers, and the understanding friends who are always there in the time of need and crisis. These superheroes wear no impenetrable suits, yet they never hesitate to face life's bullets, even though their only armor consists of the scars from previous battles often fought but not always won. In spite of their human imperfections, or maybe because of them, they never think twice about doing "the right thing," no matter the odds against them.

We all possess a superhero within, whose true home is that place of strength and hope we carry around within us every day of our lives.

That place doesn't live in our minds or our imaginations; it resides within our spirits. It's who we were created to be, what makes every life a unique work of living art instead of a two-dimensional imitation of life.

It's what makes us superheroes in a world full of victims.

* * *

I'm getting closer to home on this seemingly endless drive, and as I think about all the things that have come before this point, this present here and now, and all that awaits me up

ahead, I realize that I've been missing something I had completely forgotten about. Just before leaving Susan's, I grabbed a second cup of coffee, an extra "one for the road," which has been patiently waiting for me to remember it.

Wrapping my hand around the warm and loving cup, I toast this journey and all who have joined me on it. I drink down the dark brew with renewed zest, and it warms my soul. Susan's Best Blend has a spirit that seems to reach from the bottom of the cup. The flavor is stronger, the aroma richer, and it's just as good, if not better, than the first.

As I put the cup back into the holder on the passenger seat next to me, I notice something sticking out of my jacket pocket. It's the homemade CD Sam and Miles had burned and handed to me as I was leaving home a few days ago. They'd made it to keep me company on my ride, but in my usual rush to get wherever I thought I had to be going fast, I pushed it into my coat pocket, and that was that until just now.

It strikes me that this was something created out of love *for* me, by those created out of love *from* me. The thought warms me even more as the CD player accepts the gift from my hand. As I take another sip of Susan's coffee, one of my favorite songs begins to play. Glancing down at the illuminated display on the player, it simply reads: No Title. I recognize it only as "The Superman

Song," but I believe the group Five for Fighting performed it. Great song, great band, but what's most important is the knowledge that my sons chose *this one* just for me because they've always been Spiderman boys.

I can't repeat the lyrics exactly, but the song is about some guy running down a street, wearing a red sheet, and looking silly while searching for answers, searching for what's good inside him.

And so, with Dad's Mix surrounding me, and Susan's Blend warming me from within, I'm suddenly aware that, without realizing it, I have already zigzagged my way to the end of the highway and have never felt closer to home.

It's late at night and I feel as if I've traveled a lifetime. . . . Now, at last! The headlights of my car sweep across the darkened windows of our house as I turn into the driveway. Most of the lights are off when I enter my home and drop my suitcase and laptop by the door. For now, all I can think about is getting downstairs where I hear welcoming, familiar sounds floating up from below. My footsteps sound as heavy as they feel, trudging down those stairs, but then my step quickens as I close the distance to Miles and Sam, greeting me at the bottom with my hero's welcome, filled with hugs and "I love you's."

As my two Boy Wonders lead me back into the TV room, I know that "Dad" is the role I'm most at home with. I also know that it really doesn't matter what we're watching tonight, or if we'll even be able to stay awake for the entire movie. What matters most is having this time together and that we realize how much that means to one another without even having to say so.

Being careful not to obscure the view of their favorite superhero slinging webs across the television screen in front of us, I stretch out on the floor. Putting pen to paper, I continue my line of work, once again making sure that a short, bald, big-nosed character named Ziggy continues his journey and arrives on time each morning for the people who love him, too.

Journal Entry

Today

There once was a beautiful angel who would lay her head upon my bare chest as the fierce tempo of our beating hearts began to meet the cadence of our recovering breaths. She would tell me that there were oceans inside me while I luxuriated in stroking her long, silken hair.

It's moments such as those that define true love for us, moments that become timeless and belong to our God part at our center.

At the very end of her life, the angel looked up to me from her deathbed and smiled.

"I know nothing, Tommy," she said.

And at that moment, poised between the shadowy nothing between heaven and earth . . .

The angel knew Everything.

OK 10/10
CG 6/14
Ter 8/17
CG 5/18